SWIMMING

Titles in The History of Sports series include:

SWIMMING

BY MARTHA CAPWELL FOX

LUCENT
BOOKS

THOMSON
———★——— ™
GALE

San Diego • Detroit • New York • San Francisco • Cleveland • New Haven, Conn. • Waterville, Maine • London • Munich

THOMSON
$*$ ™
GALE

© 2003 by Lucent Books. Lucent Books is an imprint of The Gale Group, Inc.,
a division of Thomson Learning, Inc.

Lucent Books® and Thomson Learning™ are trademarks used herein under license.

For more information, contact
Lucent Books
27500 Drake Rd.
Farmington Hills, MI 48331-3535
Or you can visit our Internet site at http://www.gale.com

LIBRARY OF CONGRESS CATALOGING-IN-PUBLICATION DATA

Fox, Martha Capwell.
    Swimming / by Martha Capwell Fox.
        p. cm. — (History of sports)
Includes bibliographical references and index.
Summary: Discusses the origins and evolution of the sport of swimming, including
the different types of events, the role of women in the sport, key figures, and
problems facing the sport.
    ISBN 1-59018-073-9 (hardback : alk. paper)
    1. Swimming—Juvenile literature. [1. Swimming.] I. Title. II. Series.
    GV837 .6 .F69 2003
    797.2'1—dc21
                                                                          2002015271

Printed in the United States of America

Contents

FOREWORD

More than many areas of human endeavor, sports give us the opportunity to see the possibilities in our physical selves. As participants, we all too quickly find limits to how fast we can run, how high we can jump, how far and straight we can hit a golf ball. But as spectators we can surpass those limits as we view the accomplishments of others and see how fast, how smooth, and how strong a human being can be. We marvel at the gravity-defying leaps of a Michael Jordan as he strains toward a basketball hoop or at the dribbling of a Mia Hamm as she eludes defenders on the soccer field. We shake our heads in disbelief at the talents of a young Tiger Woods hitting an approach shot to the green or the speed of a Carl Lewis as he appears to glide around an Olympic track.

These are what the sports media call "the oohs and ahhs" of sports—the stuff of highlight reels and *Sports Illustrated* covers. But to understand a sport only in the context of its most artistic modern athletes is shortsighted, for it does little justice to the accomplishments of the athletes or to the sport itself. Far more wise is to view a sport as a continuum—a constantly moving, evolving process. On this continuum are not only the superstars of today, but the people who first played the sport, who thought about rules and strategies that would make it more challenging to play as well as a delight to watch.

Lucent Books' series The History of Sports provides such a continuum. Each book explores the development of a sport from its basic roots onward, and tries to answer questions that a reader might wonder about. Who were its first players, and what sorts of rules did the sport have then? What kinds of equipment were used in the beginning and what changes have taken place over the years?

Each title in The History of Sports also identifies key individuals in the sport's history—people whose leadership or skills have made a difference in the way the sport is played today. Included will be the easily recognized names, the Mia Hamms and the Sammy Sosas, the Wilt Chamberlains and the Wilma Rudolphs. But there are also the names of past greats, people like baseball's King Kelly, soccer's Sir Stanley Matthews, and basketball's Hank Luisetti—who may be less familiar today, but were as synonymous with their sports at one time as the "oohs and ahhs" players of today.

Finally, the series looks at the aspects of a sport that are particularly important in its current point on the continuum. Baseball today is better understood knowing about salary caps and union negotiators. One cannot truly know modern soccer without knowing about the specter of fan violence at matches. And learning about the role of instant replay is critical to a thorough understanding of today's professional football games. In viewing a sport as a continuum, the strides that have been made along the way are that much more admirable. It is a richer view, and one that shows how yesterday's limits have been surpassed—and how the limits of today are the possibilities of athletes in the future.

A Sport and a Science

If one or two of the best swimmers from 1903 suddenly materialized at a world championship meet today, they would be amazed by the sparkling pool, the split-hundredths-of-a-second timing, the body-revealing suits on the swimmers, and most of all, by the swimming itself. They would see three strokes—crawl (now known as freestyle), breaststroke, and backstroke—that are swum in a drastically different way now, and one—butterfly—which did not even exist a century ago. Most startling of all would be the speeds. Today's swimmers are so much faster, stronger, and more efficient than swimmers were one hundred years ago, they would seem almost superhuman to visitors from 1903.

One hundred years ago, even the best swimmers had very little concept of good stroke mechanics. The world's best swimmers in 1903, the Australians, had learned a time-honored overarm windmill stroke from their Polynesian neighbors, but they knew only that their way of swimming was faster than that of their English and European competitors. They may have considered theirs a better way to swim (which it was), but they did not know why that was so. The Australians, who were swimming at the then blinding pace of one hundred yards in 60.5 seconds, also did not know that they had finally set swimming on course to develop into the sport it is today.

Once the Australians had introduced the world to the crawl stroke, swimming

9

Over the past century, swimming has evolved into an intensely competitive sport.

took its first steps toward efficiency in the water. Since then, swimmers and coaches have had two goals—faster swimming and more efficient swimming.

While the fastest swimmer is not always the most efficient one in any given race, over the long haul it is efficiency in the water that ultimately yields consistent, peak performances. An efficient swimmer—one who is slicing through the water with the smoothest stroke, creating the least water resistance, and using the water to get the most forward momentum for the least physical effort possible—is probably a fast swimmer.

Only a little more than one hundred years ago, most swimmers thought that grace and efficiency in the water were mutually exclusive. Most opted for grace and thus were slow swimmers who tired easily in the water. The strokes which were then considered more efficient (if less graceful) were both slow and exhausting as well. The great achievement of twentieth-century swimming was that, for the first time in history, humans learned how to propel themselves more efficiently through the water.

Swimming has come a long way as both a competitive sport and a leisure activity in the past one hundred years. The story of its development is interwoven with many of the social and economic changes that also occurred during the past century.

Competitive swimming was an early arena for women dedicated to equal rights for their gender, and swimmers were among the first female athletic stars. In the mid–twentieth century, synchronized swimming became the first sport organized largely by and for women.

Movies, and later, television, allowed more and more people to watch the world's best swimmers and inspired countless adults and children to try to emulate them. As swimming gained popularity and prestige, it transformed from merely an amateur sport and leisure activity into a multi-million-dollar professional business, just as many other sports have done.

In the twenty-first century, swimming faces some new challenges. One is illegal performance-enhancing drug use, or "doping." There is disagreement in the sport about how widespread the practice is; random surprise drug tests among elite international competitors have caught fewer than a dozen swimmers, though among them were two Olympic gold medalists. Most swimming experts believe the sport

The growing popularity of water sports allows many people the chance to swim professionally.

is relatively clean but, given the high stakes for success, they concede that some swimmers and coaches will use every advantage they can find, no matter how risky or unethical.

Swimming's other major challenge is to broaden its appeal and participation. Since the time competitive swimming began in the nineteenth century, it has been almost entirely the sport of relatively wealthy white people. International swimming stars from South America, South Asia, and Africa are few and far between. Swimmers from the nations which traditionally have been the swimming powerhouses—the United States, Australia, Great Britain, and Canada—have been overwhelmingly white and middle class. This is because swimming pools are very expensive to build and maintain, which limits their availability in many poor urban neighborhoods and schools which have mostly minority populations. The "complexion" of swimming is slowly changing in the United States due to growing affluence among African Americans and more attention being paid to urban school and swim club programs in cities such as Atlanta and Philadelphia. The next step will be to include the rest of the world.

Swimming is now recognized as a sport that a person can enjoy and perform well throughout life. U.S. Masters meets routinely have competitors in the 90–95 age-group, and people of all ages swim in aquatics programs all over the country. Swimming counts more active participants than any other sport in the United States.

The most fascinating question about swimming in the twenty-first century is "How much faster?" There is no question that swimmers can go faster still; the limits on human swimming are still unknown. Today, children can and do swim faster than many of the sport's best of a century ago. Women's records now equal men's marks set in the late 1960s and early 1970s, and times for both sexes continue their steady downward trend. All of this has happened because coaches, swimmers, and swimming science researchers found ways—the angle of a hand, the flex of a foot—to swim each stroke just a bit more efficiently. Now swimming science has focused some of its attention on how fish and marine mammals swim. Perhaps the most significant development in swimming in the next hundred years will be humans actually learning to "swim like a fish."

CHAPTER 1

The Evolution of Competitive Swimming

Humans have been swimming for thousands of years. An eleven-thousand-year-old wall carving found in a Libyan oasis is probably the world's oldest picture of swimmers. But people have been propelling themselves through the water—for sport, for food, for warfare, for religious ritual, and just for fun—even longer.

When and where swimming began is unknown. William Wilson, a nineteenth-century scholar of swimming, believed that swimming is one of the oldest human skills, developed (or discovered) long before humankind had any way of recording it. Even after writing was invented, no one appears to have put down any instructions for faster, easier ways to swim. Swimming technique, such as it was, was taught by word of mouth and example. Early "strokes" were probably nothing more than simple movements that came naturally to people in the water.

Swimmers have always raced each other, but there is no evidence that there were any organized swimming races in the ancient world. Swimming was not part of the original Olympic Games, which featured only running and throwing events. Greek and Roman soldiers who were trained to swim probably competed to show off their skills, but if military swim meets occurred, no one thought them important enough to record. If there were army or navy manuals of swimming, as there were for other military skills, none have survived. Finally, with the fall of the Roman Empire, clean water became scarce and swimming fell into such disfavor that it all but disappeared in Europe for a thousand years.

Japan: The Birthplace of Scientific Swimming

On the other side of the world, in Japan, swimming has a far different history. Interscholastic swimming competition in Japan has existed since 1603, and it was made an organized school sport by imperial edict shortly after.

Since Japan is surrounded by the ocean and dotted with large inland lakes and rivers, as many as twelve distinct styles of swimming evolved, each suited to different conditions. Each form of swimming had its own name and was developed to adapt to various types of water.

WHY PEOPLE STOPPED SWIMMING

Swimming pretty much disappeared in Europe after the fall of the Roman Empire in the fifth century. The early Christian church took a dim view of the Romans' "immoral" focus on bathing and the body and condemned the luxurious public and private baths as sites for indecency and sin. Being nude—the way everyone swam in the ancient world—became shameful.

Clean water was a casualty of the Empire's collapse, as well. Bodies of water began to be looked on—correctly—as places where diseases started and were spread. Swimming went from being a healthful physical, and even spiritual, exercise to a mortal danger. When people did swim, they were careful to keep their heads above the water and used a kind of breaststroke or dog paddle. Swimming skills disappeared, and drowning became a common way of death.

For about the next twelve hundred years, most Europeans were nonswimmers. Swimming did not become acceptable

The excavations at Pompeii and other early cities led to the discovery of ancient swimming pools.

again until the eighteenth century, when excavations at Pompeii and other parts of the ancient world sparked a fascination with everything Greek and Roman. Educated upper-class gentlemen, especially in Britain and France, were eager to imitate their ancient heroes and enthusiastically embraced swimming. In America, Benjamin Franklin preached the joys and benefits of swimming, and by the mid–nineteenth century, people were back in the water.

For instance, Japanese swimmers developed a kind of breaststroke for swimming long distances in the open ocean, and another for swimming upstream in rivers. The samurai, the warrior aristocrats of Japan, learned to swim carrying weapons and invented a kicking technique that allowed them to shoot arrows while in the water. This was the first time that swimming technique was analyzed and modified to meet specific goals. Thus it can be said that swimming sports science began in Japan.

Apart from its military uses, swimming played an important part in Japan's religious and ceremonial rituals. Ancient Japanese accounts of swimming races which were part of religious celebrations go back as far as 36 B.C. The samurai, for whom physical and mental self-control were major aspects of their religious practice, showed off these skills in pageant-like shows of slow, synchronized strokes across Lake Hamana, the center of elite Japanese swim training. Until after World War II, the national championships were held in a pool near a major religious shrine; the meet was followed by a solemn procession of the athletes and their coaches to the shrine.

Early Japanese swimmers apparently were fast, strong, and efficient, but since Japan was isolated from the world until the mid–nineteenth century, Japanese swimming skills never spread beyond the island nation. On the other hand, skills and techniques developed in Australia, Europe, and the United States had little influence on Japanese swimming until well into the twentieth century. When the Japanese first entered the international competition scene at the 1920 Olympics, they were defeated in every event. The techniques which drove them through all kinds of rough open waters were not as efficient in the relative calm of the racing pool.

Britain Takes the Lead

In the West, organized swimming races did not begin until the 1830s. In 1837, John Strachan, a London wine merchant, created the National Swimming Society. Strachan sponsored the first race to be written up in a newspaper, a short thrash between two swimmers which took place in the Serpentine, a lake in London's Hyde Park. That first race, held on August 5, 1837, was so successful for Strachan that he quickly put on several others. The first competitive swimmers were professionals in the sense that they competed for a monetary prize, but they were probably not very skilled swimmers nor the most savory members of society. Neither were the people who came to watch.

The National Swimming Society's events were held only so the spectators could gamble. Swimmers were regarded the same as racehorses, fighting cocks, racing dogs, and prizefighters—merely something to

WHAT MAKES A POOL "FAST"?

Some pools, like the Indiana Natatorium in Indianapolis and the Olympic Pool in Sydney, Australia, have a reputation for being "fast." This actually means they are more than just pools where records are set regularly and great performances put in. Swimming speed actually can be *built* into a pool.

Tim Minnich, public information director of the Indiana Natatorium, explains in a 2001 interview how such a pool is designed. There are four major factors in a fast pool—depth, surface gutters, wave-damping lane lines, and water circulation on the bottom. "It has to be fairly deep; seven to nine feet is ideal. This lets the turbulence go down and not rebound back up to the surface," he says. "The other reason for the pool to be deep is to have the water recirculate along the bottom; that way the filtered water gets back in the pool without creating a current."

Lap swimmers of all levels have benefited from lane lines that break up the wakes and waves kicked up by swimmers in other lanes. The ones used in top competition pools have plastic floats with flat fins called "vanes" that break up waves to keep them from both crossing into another lane and rebounding back into the swimmer. This not only means that competitors do not have to battle through each other's turbulence, says Minnich. Lane lines keep racers from "catching a draft"—getting towed along by the pull of the swimmer just ahead of them.

Fast pools have wide, shallow, water-level gutters all the way around the peri-meter. This also absorbs waves and turbulence and keeps the water from just slapping the wall and rebounding back into the pool.

Of course, outstanding performances are to be expected at the championship meets that take place in pools like this, and most of their "fast" reputation is due to swimmers who rise to the occasion. But having the perfect pool for the race of a lifetime does not hurt.

wager on. The people who came to these early events had little or no interest in the sport itself—only in whether or not the outcome paid off for them. Nevertheless, gambling on these swimming races made them very popular.

Within a year Strachan renamed his organization the British Swimming Society and began to stage races in several English cities. He also expanded the number of swimmers to as many as twelve per race, reasoning that more swimmers to bet on would attract in more spectators. Strachan also created the concept of a "champion"—the winner of several different races, who would collect a big prize and a valuable medal. Strachan was the first sports organizer to use this term in relation to a sport. While Strachan was expanding the scope of his swimming competitions, several social conditions in Britain were beginning to steer competitive swimming toward its modern form.

In the boarding schools where Britain's elite young men were educated, swimming was increasingly in vogue. Ancient legends and stories about Greek and Roman swimming heroes sparked a passion for swimming. The poet Lord Byron went so far as to swim the Hellespont, the narrow but treacherous strait between Europe and Asia, in homage to his hero Leander who was said to have made the dangerous swim nightly to visit his true love, Hero. The healthfulness and the supposed character-building discipline of swimming in cold water appealed to upperclass Victorians. So the sport—both as a solo endeavor and a group competition—was greatly encouraged at the top schools such as Eton and Harrow, and the sons of wealthy Britons enthusiastically took up the sport in nearby ponds and rivers.

In the crowded, squalid industrial cities swimming was being promoted for another reason. Social reformers and early medical researchers became convinced that the physical and spiritual ills of what they considered the "lower classes" could be relieved by providing them with clean water for drinking and bathing. This triggered government passage of several laws that forced cities to provide sanitary water and public facilities for swimming, bathing, and doing laundry. By 1852 the eight public baths in London, virtually all of which were constructed in poor areas, were being used by over eight hundred thousand people a year. So while the rich were still swimming in open water outdoors, less privileged Englishmen flocked to the first indoor public swimming pools of modern times.

An eighteenth-century engraving depicts Leander swimming the Hellespont.

Standardized Swimming

As more people learned to swim and more races were held both in pools and open water, the popularity of competitive swimming grew in Britain throughout the second half of the nineteenth century. Several different organizations tried to set rules and standards both for races and the status of the swimmers as either professional or amateur. Race promoters found that shorter indoor races attracted more competitors. Since early pools were of all different sizes, it became apparent that standardized distances for pool races would have to be set. The invention of affordable stopwatches in the 1860s made it possible to accurately time a swim and standardized timing as well.

Eventually, the Amateur Swimming Association (ASA), which spun off of the Amateur Athletic Association, gained control of swimming competition in Britain. The directors of the ASA quickly learned a great deal about governing and promoting a competitive sport. This gave them a lot of influence in the revival of the Olympics in 1896 and in getting swimming included in the Games. The ASA's experiences with setting ethical standards and rules of competition eventually formed the basis for the international swimming sanctioning body. This organization, the Federation Internationale de Natation Amateur, or FINA, remains the official governing body of swimming.

Despite the flux in the administration of the sport, interest spread to Europe, North America, and especially to Australia. It was from Australia that the biggest breakthrough in swimming technique came, just in time for swimming's debut on the international sports scene.

WHO RUNS SWIMMING?

Competitive swimming is organized by local, regional, national, and international organizations. The world governing body is the International Federation of Amateur Swimming, which is universally known by its initials in French, FINA. It is FINA which sanctions the meets that decide national and international championships as well as Olympic trials; FINA's standards for drug testing and allowable drug usage are generally accepted by Olympic and other race-sanctioning bodies.

FINA is made up of all the national governing bodies, including United States Swimming, Inc. USS was formed in 1980, when Congress effectively broke up the AAU (Amateur Athletic Union) by forbidding any sports-sanctioning body from controlling more than five sports. USS's age-group club program, from which virtually all elite American swimmers come, is the biggest swimming program in the United States.

The National Collegiate Athletic Association regulates college swimming, while the National Interscholastic Swimming Coaches Association governs high school meets. The YMCA, which has taught more people to swim than any other organization in the world, is also a large presence in American swimming with its youth competition program. In addition, many YMCAs have U.S. Masters teams, though Masters competition (which is open to people over nineteen) is governed by USS.

A woman cuts through the water using the stroke that used to be called the Australian crawl.

The Australian Crawl: Efficiency Comes to Swimming

By modern standards, the best British, European, and American swimmers in the nineteenth century were extraordinarily slow. Even the fastest, most skilled swimmers were so inefficient that they could keep up a fast pace for only one to two hundred yards before they were too exhausted to continue.

Western swimmers used a kind of elegant but slow breaststroke, though by the late nineteenth century, many had adopted the trudgen, an overarm stroke coupled with a frog kick. But all swimmers held their heads above the surface, which dropped their legs and torsos low in the water. This caused them to pull their bodies through the water against their own resistance, an exhausting and inefficient way to swim.

By the beginning of the twentieth century, Australian swimmers had abandoned the slow European techniques and adopted the swift windmill stroke of their Polynesian neighbors. Modern speed swimming's real birthplace was in the Pacific's towering breakers, says legendary Canadian swimming coach and historian, Cecil Colwin, in his book *Breakthrough Swimming*.

Polynesians had bodysurfed for thousands of years, and they learned to combine fast, flailing arm strokes with a flutter kick (in which the swimmer rapidly whips the legs alternately up and down) to catch and ride the crests of the waves. Oral history from many different areas of the South Pacific suggests that long-distance swims between islands may have been common as well.

The Cavill brothers—Dick, Syd, and Arthur—revolutionized swimming with this fast, efficient stroke, which became known as the Australian crawl. Dick Cavill lowered the 100-yard record to 58.6 seconds in 1900. Five years later, American Charles Daniels boosted the kick rate from two or four beats to six beats per stroke and completely rewrote the record books until he retired from competition in 1910. Using the Australian crawl, Daniels won gold medals at the St. Louis Olympics in 1904, the "unofficial" Athens Games in 1906, and the 1908 Olympics in London.

Keeping Up the Speed

By speeding up his kicking rate, Daniels, who was a superb natural athlete, had unwittingly tapped into the principle of continuous propulsion. Prior to this, all swimming strokes had a pause at some point in the stroke, during which the swimmer's forward momentum slowed or even stopped. This caused swimmers to continually restart their forward progress, which slowed them and wasted their energy. But

when Daniels coordinated the arm stroke with a constant kick, he never stopped going forward. In addition, the steady kick helped hold his lower body nearly flat and close to the surface.

THE BEST THING TO HAPPEN TO SWIMMING

Coaches and scholars of swimming agree on one thing: The development of the swim goggle is the most important thing to happen to swimming since the 1970s—and maybe in the entire history of the sport. Introduced in 1969, goggles allowed coaches to extend workouts until they were satisfied with the results instead of having to release swimmers whose eyes were so burnt and blurred with chlorine they could no longer see. Longer workouts led directly to major drops in competitive times, especially in the longer events in the 1970s, as every serious swimmer adopted goggles.

Today, goggles come in a huge variety of shapes, materials, and colors; swimmers can choose from goggles designed for sprint races, long races, open water swims, and practices. Nearsighted swimmers can get their glasses prescription put into goggle lenses, which lets them see when they lift their heads out of the water. Underwater, goggles give near-perfect vision to even the most myopic, which is their other great benefit for swimmers.

Savvy readers can date a swimming book by the pictures—if the swimmers have no goggles, it is almost certain the book was published before 1975.

This was the biggest technical breakthrough in the modern history of swimming. Cecil Colwin writes in *Breakthrough Swimming*:

> [Crawl] was the fastest stroke ever developed, and it highlighted the fact that a swimmer must produce continuous propulsion to maintain an even velocity.... The first crawl stroke pioneers learned the importance of streamlining, that we swim faster by reducing drag.... It quickly became apparent that coordination was most important, especially in reference to maintaining continuous propulsion.[1]

Breathing technique was another hurdle that had to be overcome in the quest for speed. Again, coaches and swimmers turned to the South Pacific islanders, who had long used a method of turning their heads out of the water to breathe every few strokes. By the 1920 Olympics, this technique was almost universally used. However, like every other aspect of what was becoming freestyle, there have been long arguments since then about the finer points of breathing—how often, turning versus lifting the head, whether to breathe on each side, and many others.

Throughout the twentieth century, advances in underwater photography and other tools to watch and record the actions of elite swimmers yielded greater understanding of the biomechanics of swimming. Each major discovery led to refinements in freestyle technique, some as subtle as the hand's angle when it enters the water, others as obvious as the change from holding the body flat and rigid to allowing the torso to roll from side to side on each stroke. Each discovery also triggered controversy. And each discovery that has paid off in the pool with broken records and gold medals has rapidly been copied and adopted by most, if not all, swimmers.

Currently, most coaches and swimming sports scientists believe that the hallmarks of the best swimmers are efficient streamlining of the body (constantly presenting as little resistance as possible), a long stroke length (or distance per stroke), and a fast stroke rate. According to Cecil Colwin:

> At the 2000 Sydney Olympics, the advanced swimming styles of freestyle champions Pieter van den Hoogenband, Ian Thorpe, Gary Hall, Jr., and Alexander Popov were seen as a breakthrough to a new paradigm of stroke mechanics. Based on the skilled use of the principle of momentum, their easy gliding action ... showed the world of swimming that accurate timing and efficient streamlining produces momentum in the most efficient way to overcome resistance.[2]

THE SKINSUIT: THE EMPEROR'S NEW SWIMSUIT?

During the twentieth century, racers' swimsuits evolved from covering most of the swimmer's body to revealing most of it. By the 1996 Atlanta Olympics, racing suits were so sheer and skimpy that television cameras focused on swimmers from only the shoulders up whenever they could. Four years later, however, swimmers at Sydney were at least half covered up. They wore skinsuits, the skintight swimwear ranging from a pair of pants to a tank suit with longer legs or full-length legs, to a suit reaching from neck to wrists to ankles.

The rationale behind each design—and each manufacturer's claims—is the same. The suits, made of "miracle" fabrics (which may also increase buoyancy), turn the sleekest swimmer even sleeker. That brings them two giant steps closer to the Holy Grail of swimming: reduced drag. Reduced drag adds up to more speed.

Do the suits really make a difference? A lot of swimmers have broken records while wearing

Wearing a skinsuit, Ian Thorpe celebrates after winning the gold medal in the men's 400-meter freestyle.

them. But some researchers say that a lot of records have been broken by racers in conventional suits, even while they were competing against swimmers in skinsuits. Some well-controlled scientific studies, which used flume pools (in which a swimmer strokes against a steady current of water) found no difference in drag or resistance between the skinsuits and regular ones.

At the elite level, even thousandths of a second can make the difference between winning and losing. Right now, there is no evidence that skinsuits definitely *do not* make a difference. For the average competitor, however, good training, good nutrition, and a good attitude probably make more difference than an expensive skin suit.

Stroke Developments

Freestyle is not the only stroke that has gone through a long evolution in search of speed and efficiency. The other three strokes —breaststroke, butterfly, and backstroke— have all been studied, experimented with, and significantly changed in the past one hundred years.

Breaststroke

Breaststroke was the style Europeans favored until the early 1900s. In the nineteenth century, breaststrokers tended to pull their legs up close to their chests, then push out sharply. This broke their momentum, because drawing the legs forward while pushing the arms back moves each end of the body in opposite directions simultaneously. Breaststrokers also tended to keep their arms close to the surface and to sweep them wide and flat. By the 1920s Louis de Breda Handley, who coached many female champions at the Women's Swimming Association of New York, improved the stroke by teaching his swimmers to take a shorter stroke that pulled down as well as out. He also devised the alternate kick/stroke technique, which brought continuous propulsion to breaststroke for the first time.

From the 1930s until 1956, breaststroke was often swum in a hybrid called the breaststroke-butterfly. This developed when American Henry Myers discovered in 1933 that he could swim faster than the fastest breaststroker on his team when he combined the breaststroke kick with a double overarm stroke. Much to his and his coach's surprise, there was nothing in the rules which prevented him from racing this way. This led to twenty years of confusion as the hybrid stroke evolved into modern butterfly and classic breaststroke almost disappeared from major competition. In 1956, FINA, the world governing body of swimming, agreed with the International Olympic Committee on rules that established butterfly as a separate stroke, and breaststroke began to regain its identity.

By the 1960s, there were two approaches to breaststroke. The flat breaststroke, favored by Americans and Russians, tended to keep the body nearly flat and rigid in the water. Most other swimmers preferred a "wave" stroke, which allowed the swimmer's body to rise and fall in the water with the motion of the stroke. University of Michigan head coach John Urbanchek explains:

> The main difference between the flat breaststroke and the wave is that the flat stroke is driven by the feet and legs (rear-wheel drive) while the wave breaststroke is driven by the lower arms (front-wheel drive). The wave stroke is more energy efficient because it reduces the deceleration between the arm pull and the leg drive. The arms give the initial speed, the upper body lunges forward and the kick follows

shortly thereafter. The three continuous movements result in a smooth, wave-like appearance.[3]

Development of the so-called wave technique was hampered by a rule that prevented breaststrokers from ducking their heads fully under the surface. When this rule was rescinded in the late 1980s, the wave action breaststroke gained ascendancy, and American Mike Barrowman reset most of the international records with his mastery of the technique. The "pull-lunge-kick" sequence of the wave action technique, which has become standard in breaststroke competition, is the most efficient method of the stroke devised so far, assuring that the swimmer maintains constant forward propulsion.

Butterfly

While freestyle is the fastest stroke, butterfly is the second-fastest. Though it looks exhausting (and is for swimmers who have not mastered the technique), proficient butterfliers are capable of swimming long distances using only that stroke. Butterfly has even been used in long open water swims; Gail Rice used the stroke exclusively on a swim in 1997 from Bimini, an island in the Bahamas, to Miami, and it is Chicago-based Tom Boetcher's signature stroke for three-mile races in Lake Michigan.

The butterfly was not synonymous with efficiency until Jack Sieg, a swimmer at the University of Iowa, devised the dolphin kick to combine with the double overarm stroke in 1935. (A swimmer doing the dolphin kick keeps his or her legs pressed together with the knees slightly bent and kicks in one continuous motion from hips to toes.) However, this combination did not pass the regulatory hurdles until 1956, so swimmers and coaches did not begin tinkering with the stroke until the early 1960s. After research and observation showed that the butterflier's body moves around a fulcrum centered just below his or her hips, a movement called "short-axis rotation," stroke technique began to focus on coordinating the timing and movement of the arms with a double downward kick. The double kick enables the swimmer to maintain forward motion while the arms and upper body are out of the water. Other coaches say a single kick is sufficient, provided it is the starting point of a wave of forward movement which picks up all the power of the swimmer's muscles from the feet through the legs and hips and into the torso.

One firm believer in the power of this short-axis rotation in butterfly is Terry Laughlin, former head swimming coach at the United States Military Academy and developer of a widely respected adult instruction program called Total Immersion. "The body undulation [wavelike motion]

A woman propels herself through the water using the breaststroke. Advances in various swim styles have resulted in greater human efficiency in the water.

of butterfly works the same way as double-poling on skis. Instead of muscling your arms back, you should begin each stroke by anchoring your hands far in front of your shoulders, then using your core muscles—somewhat in the manner of a stomach crunch—to pull your hips and legs toward that point," he says. This way the muscles of the torso become the link between the propulsive power of the legs and the forward reach of the hands and arms. "When you learn to use your arms to 'hold your place' in the water and let your torso do the work, enormous power

is produced with relatively little effort," Laughlin says.[4]

Backstroke

A fourth swimming stroke is backstroke, any movement performed in water by a swimmer floating on his or her back. A skilled backstroker has to learn much more than how to swim fast without seeing where he or she is going.

There are a few different kinds of backstroke, but the term is most commonly used for a stroke that looks, on the surface, like freestyle done backward. This is not the case, though. The structure of the human shoulder keeps backstroke from being the exact opposite of freestyle. Even the most talented, flexible, and athletic backstrokers cannot stroke down and under their backs the way freestylers do under their fronts. Thus, several variations on arm technique have been tried.

In the 1936 Berlin Olympics, Chicago high schooler Adolph Keifer took the 100-meter medal with a straight-arm stroke kept out to his sides and just below the surface. This was different from the past technique of reaching as deep into the water as possible. Keifer's style remained popular for about a decade. Then Allan Stack won the backstroke events in the 1948 Olympics with a bent-arm pull paired with a six-beat flutter kick. Through the 1950s, 1960s, and 1970s, backstrokers plowed through the water this way, nearly flat on their backs with their chins tucked tightly to their chests.

A faster, more fluid style appeared in the 1990s, as champions like Jeff Rouse and Lenny Krayzelburg set records with a

The backstroke technique has been modified several times to reduce drag and achieve faster times for swimmers.

body-rolling, chin-up style that keeps the body streamlined and close to the surface. The body roll allows the swimmer a greater range of arm and shoulder motion than when lying flat, and it taps the power of the hip and torso muscles for the stroke. Dick Hannula, one of the most talented coaches in American high school and club swimming, says success in backstroke relies on three factors: rhythm, relaxation, and rotation. "Rhythm facilitates power, which is the result of rotation. Rotation refers to the hip-initiated trunk rotation that generates stroking power and reduces drag," he says. "Relaxation assists in maintaining steady stroking power. Arm recovery and breathing pattern are the two main components of relaxation." [5]

An innovative racing strategy in backstroke—dolphin kicking underwater for a distance before breaking out on the surface and stroking—has helped lower times, particularly in the 50- and 100-meter events. Controversy erupted when backstrokers began using this technique during starts and after turns in the early 1990s, and some swimmers and coaches wanted it banned. A compromise was reached when a new rule, limiting the distance a swimmer could stay underwater to no more than fifteen meters, was put in place in the mid-1990s.

Science in Swimming

Advances in swimming have been closely tied to advances in the technologies which make it possible to study humans while they swim. Underwater photography and videography allow coaches to analyze every move underwater. Flume pools, in which a swimmer strokes against a continuous current of water, can hold a swimmer in place and reveal how much drag and resistance he or she creates. Advances in nutrition, orthopedics, and physiology have all combined to make swimmers faster. Some scientists suspect that it is not possible to lower swim times much further. Others say that, given the combination of training, advances in nutrition, and the careful selection of talented youngsters, swimming may still see significant reductions in record times

CHAPTER 2

Extreme Swimming: Open Water Races and Solo Swims

Until about 150 years ago, all swim races—all swimming, for that matter—happened in the open water of rivers, lakes, and oceans. People who wanted to swim simply accepted cold water, powerful currents, choppy waves, and the occasional threat from marine life as part of the experience.

Timing and distance both were imprecise in early open water races, most of which were less than one thousand yards long. Events were point-to-point, with the winner being the first person to reach the destination. Even after indoor races became more standardized, public interest in open water swim races and fascination with great feats of endurance in the water remained. Still, the interest was usually in gambling on the outcome, not the sport itself.

First Across the Channel

In his quest to be the first person to swim across the English Channel between England and France, Matthew Webb turned that fondness for betting to his own advantage. Webb was already famous in Britain for several extraordinary feats in the water, particularly a daring though unsuccessful rescue attempt on the high seas in 1873. While serving on a Cunard steamship, Webb dove into a roiling ocean to retrieve a sailor who had been swept overboard. Though he could not find the lost man, Webb himself survived nearly an hour in the icy Atlantic until being picked up and returned to the safety of the ship.

Webb realized that swimming from England to France would require intense preparation and a fair amount of money. He set himself some highly publicized swimming challenges, such as an eighteen-mile swim down the Thames River and laid large bets on himself. He not only collected his money, but attracted the attention of investors who funded his training and set up a large money prize should he succeed.

On August 24, 1875, Webb entered the water from the Admiralty Pier in Dover, the point in England closest to the French coast twenty-one miles away. This was his second attempt in less than two weeks; on August 12, after spending nearly seven hours in the water, weather had forced Webb to abort his first attempt after covering only about five miles of the distance. In contrast, the weather on August 24 was flawless, and by 4 P.M. Webb had swum farther in just over three hours than he had gone in seven hours the first time.

Webb averaged a steady 1-mile-an-hour pace, and then in the middle of the night, cheered on by the passengers aboard a passing ferry and pushed by a steady current, he picked up the pace to 1.5 miles an hour. By 3 A.M. fourteen hours after leaving Dover, Webb was four miles from his destination, Cap Griz-Nez, France. However, wind, tides, and currents pushed

him thirteen miles along the French shore toward Calais, badly slowing his forward progress. Webb's supporters and the

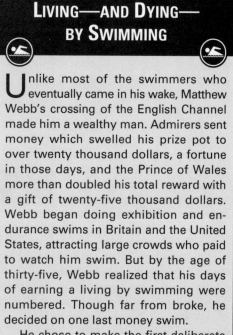

LIVING—AND DYING—BY SWIMMING

Unlike most of the swimmers who eventually came in his wake, Matthew Webb's crossing of the English Channel made him a wealthy man. Admirers sent money which swelled his prize pot to over twenty thousand dollars, a fortune in those days, and the Prince of Wales more than doubled his total reward with a gift of twenty-five thousand dollars. Webb began doing exhibition and endurance swims in Britain and the United States, attracting large crowds who paid to watch him swim. But by the age of thirty-five, Webb realized that his days of earning a living by swimming were numbered. Though far from broke, he decided on one last money swim.

He chose to make the first deliberate attempt to swim through the whirlpool in the Niagara River, downstream from the Falls. Undeterred by the fact that over eighty people had drowned in accidents on that stretch in the previous twenty-three years, Webb had himself rowed to the middle of the river at 4 P.M. on July 24, 1883. Wearing the same red silk swimming suit he had crossed the Channel in, Webb dove into the current. Ten thousand horrified spectators watched the world's most famous swimmer disappear into the maw of the whirlpool. His battered body was found three days later, still clad in tatters of red silk. The brave captain finally met a body of water he could not conquer.

WET SUITS: CHEATER OR EQUALIZER?

Most open water swimmers have firm opinions about wet suits. The purists abhor them as an "unnatural" advantage. The practical advocate them as sensible insurance against hypothermia. Generally, wet suits are banned in international competition because the rules set by FINA prohibit all flotation devices.

The real root of the argument is that wearing a wet suit makes a swimmer as much as 20 percent more buoyant, which translates into

Although wet suits are banned in most competitive events, many advocate their use for protection against hypothermia.

easier, faster swimming. Among triathletes, it is commonly conceded that a wet suit turns an average swimmer into a good one. It thus wipes out the advantage that great swimmers have over great runners and cyclists who are mediocre swimmers.

A wet suit is just a piece of equipment, retort its supporters. If wet suits (which have greatly cut down hypothermia incidents in triathlons) are banned, other equipment, such as superlight carbon fiber bikes, should be banned as well.

There are many races and sanctioned solo swims where wet suits are forbidden, such as the Manhattan Marathon, the Catalina Channel, and the English Channel.

Other races, like the Alcatraz Sharkfest in always frigid San Francisco Bay, have wet suit/no wet suit divisions. Most of the Great Lakes would be impossible to cross without a wet suit, says Jim Dreyer on www.swimjimswim.com, because of the distance as well as the temperature.

The argument may never be resolved. Most elite events will probably continue to hold the principle that the natural conditions like weather and water temperature are the same for everyone during a race, and each competitor must contend with them. In "wet suit–optional" events most swimmers wear one, which suggests that surviving to the end of the race is an even higher principle.

reporters in the small boats that accompanied him feared for his success, but with a determined marshaling of his last strength, Webb hauled himself ashore in France twenty-one hours and forty-five minutes after leaving Dover. After a meal,

he was taken to a hotel for a ten-hour sleep before he returned to England and great acclaim.

Webb's feat was not repeated until thirty-six years later, when Thomas Burgess finally succeeded in swimming the Channel in 1912 after fourteen failed attempts. Eleven years later, in the summer of 1923, three successful swims were made, including the first begun from the French shore. Then in 1926 Gertrude Ederle became the first woman to swim the Channel, smashing the old record by over an hour as well. Ederle's record—14 hours, 31 minutes—had stood for only a few weeks when German Ernst Vierkoetter, the final person to cross the Channel that remarkable summer, made the swim in 12:40.

The English Channel: The Everest of Open Water

Since then about 7,000 people have tried to swim across the Channel. Only 550 have succeeded. It is said that more people have gone into space than have swum the Channel. Though not the longest, coldest, or most dangerous open water swim, it is probably the toughest even under the best conditions of weather, wind, and water temperature.

The warmest the water ever gets is about sixty-three degrees Fahrenheit, and rules dictated by tradition prohibit use of a wet suit. Swimmers may wear only a suit, cap, and goggles. The tides and currents are strong and variable in this narrow body of water; swimmers who do not plan their route and time their swim carefully can find themselves helplessly battling shifting flows of water. The fact that

the Channel is one of the busiest shipping lanes in the world adds to the challenge; freighter and ferry wakes create large waves. While some swimmers fail to make it across because they give up, others have died, most recently a Mexican woman in 1999. Every summer, some swimmers suffer hypothermia so severe that they have to be picked up by helicopter and taken to a hospital.

Aspiring Channel swimmers have to register with the two organizations that control Channel crossings—the Channel Swimming Association and the Channel Swimming & Piloting Federation. These organizations require swimmers to meet certain standards, including a proven record in cold water long-distance swimming. Then swimmers must hire a registered Channel pilot who will steer their support boat and provide a support crew, including a doctor, for themselves. All this can cost upwards of ten thousand dollars and there is no guarantee of success. The only material prize is a Rolex watch awarded each season to the fastest crosser. As of the end of the 2002 season, the fastest crossing by a man was 7:17 in 1995 by Chad Hundeby, and the fastest by a woman, American Penny Lee Dean, 7:40, set in 1978.

The real rewards, say those who have braved the swim, are personal. "Once you have swum the Channel," says Marcia Cleveland, who did it in 1996, "no other obstacle in life seems insurmountable."[6]

The Catalina Channel Race

Other bodies of water have lured swimmers into trying to cross them, but few have been the site of events like William Wrigley's Catalina Channel race. After Gertrude Ederle swam the Channel in 1926, Wrigley, the chewing gum magnate, came up with the idea of a star-studded swimming race. Wrigley owned Santa Catalina Island, a popular summer resort twenty-two miles off the coast of Southern California. His race had two aims—to pour money into his businesses on the island and to link his gum to the vigorous athletic image of the swimmers.

Wrigley wanted his race to be even more important than swimming the English Channel, so he offered forty thousand dollars in prize money, an enormous amount for the 1920s. Twenty-five thousand dollars would go to the first swimmer to reach the breakwater at San Vincente, a point with a lighthouse on the Palos Verdes peninsula. In addition, fifteen thousand dollars would go to the first woman to finish. (Apparently, no one expected a woman to finish first overall.)

MANHATTAN ISLAND MARATHON

The first recorded swim around Manhattan Island, New York, was in 1915 by seventeen-year-old Robert Dowling. During the 1920s, Charlotte Schoemmel made the circle and set records several times. But by the 1950s and 1960s, no one willingly set foot in either the East or Hudson Rivers, both dangerously polluted. When Diana Nyad made her solo circuit around the island in 1975, she was immunized against as many toxins as there were shots for. Still, she reported having to dodge all sorts of distasteful flotsam and jetsam, including, it has been said, a dead dog.

Pollution was still a concern, though less so, when the first Manhattan Island Marathon was held in 1981. Since then the waters around New York City have improved to the point that there are no safety warnings about the water for the racers, other than the standard one of not swallowing it.

Though purists consider it something of an "assisted" race, since swimmers ride the tide up the East River and the current down the Hudson, the swim around Manhattan lures the top open water swimmers. One attraction is the distance—a challenging 28.5 miles. Another is the media exposure. With only about twenty solo racers and another thirty to forty people on relay teams, each swimmer, especially the winner, gets a lot of attention in the biggest media center in the world. A third attraction is the experience itself. "Where else can you swim past some of the world's best-known landmarks?" says open water veteran and New York City resident Patricia Sener in an October 2002 interview. "You get to see the city from a perspective that few people ever do. And it's gorgeous."

Unfortunately for many of the swimmers who hoped to vie for the prize, the race was held on January 15, 1927, because Wrigley's strategy was to bring business to Catalina Island at the depths of the off-season. The water temperature was in the mid-fifties, deterring more than half the four hundred entrants from ever entering the water. In all, 102 swimmers (including a legless teenage newspaper boy from San Francisco) took the start, among them some of North America's finest swimmers.

Eight and a half hours into the race, only twenty competitors were left. Among the dropouts were Henry Sullivan and Charles Toth, both Channel veterans, and Charlotte Schoemmel, the record holder for swimming around Manhattan. Out in front, still swimming at a phenomenal pace of nearly two miles an hour, was seventeen-year-old Canadian champion George Young. Dogging him twenty yards behind was Norman Ross, twenty-six, who had won gold medals in both the 1920 and 1924 Olympics and held virtually every amateur record in American swimming.

By midnight fifteen thousand people had gathered on the point at San Vincente, overlooking the ocean. Those with cars turned on their headlights and blew their horns, and the excited murmur became a roar as they anticipated a close finish. Around 2:30 A.M. Ross's crew learned that Young expected to reach land within thirty minutes. Knowing there was no way he

Myrtle Huddleston was the first woman to swim the Catalina Channel.

could catch the young Canadian, a humiliated Ross abandoned the race. At 3:02 A.M. Young waded ashore after being in the water for fifteen hours and forty-five minutes. Three hours later, the two remaining women gave up about a mile offshore. William Wrigley magnanimously gave them twenty-five hundred dollars each.

Though most of the swimmers had failed to reach their goal, Wrigley attained his. The first Catalina Channel swim was also the world's first mass international open water race. It generated lots of business for both Catalina Island and Wrigley's Chewing Gum and was such a popular success that it launched an era of open water marathons.

Since Wrigley's race, several hundred people have swum across the San Pedro Channel, as it is known today. Many swimmers use Catalina as a rehearsal for the English Channel, since the distance and water temperature are similar.

The Canadian National Exhibition Races

Fired up by his success at Catalina, William Wrigley figured the best way to turn Canadians into gum chewers was another big swim race. The Canadian National Exhibition, an annual event that combines displays put up by major Canadian manufacturers with athletic contests, is held in Toronto on the shore of Lake Ontario. Less than two months after the Catalina Channel race, Wrigley's Gum announced it would sponsor a swim with a prize purse of $50,000, with $30,000 going to the winner. This was a staggering amount of money, equal to about $250,000 today, and stood as the largest monetary prize ever in open water competition. Not surprisingly, the event attracted the best swimmers in the world, including George Young, Norman Ross, Charlotte Schoemmel, Edward Keating, the Frenchman Georges Michel, and the new English Channel record holder, Ernst Vierkoetter.

The organizers laid out a triangular course, 2.3 miles on a side, so that the entire race would be visible from the grandstands erected on the shore. The swimmers would go around the triangle three times for a race length of 21 miles. On August 30, 1927, thirty-five thousand people paid to watch Ernst Vierkoetter, the German Channel champion, blow the Catalina winner and hometown favorite, George Young, out of the water and finish the course after eleven hours and forty-five minutes in bone-chilling fifty-one-degree water. His thirty-thousand-dollar prize stood as the largest financial bonus in swimming until the 1990s.

Because the swimming marathon became the most popular feature of the Canadian National Exhibition (CNE), it continued in various forms through the 1970s. Officials experimented with the distance, though the fifteen-mile length seemed the most popular. While the distances varied, the grueling conditions usually persisted—harsh winds, water temperatures in the forties and fifties, and wildly shifting currents make Lake Ontario one of the most difficult bodies of water to swim in.

Each year from 1949 to 1955, Canadian Cliff Lumsdon won the CNE race. Lumsdon was the finest open water swimmer of his time, winning the race around Atlantic City and the lake swims in Quebec during those years, as well as becoming the first person (and one of the few ever) to swim across the Strait of Juan de Fuca between Washington State and Vancouver Island.

Canadian Marilyn Bell swims across Lake Ontario. She was the first person to accomplish this feat.

But Lumsdon's greatest victory came in the CNE race in 1955. Canadian Marilyn Bell had become the first person to swim across Lake Ontario the previous year, so the race route was set for the same distance, starting at Saint Catharines on the south shore and finishing at the CNE fairgrounds in Toronto. Abominable weather conditions the day of the race led officials to change to a triangular course totaling thirty-two miles. After fourteen hours only Lumsdon remained in the forty-nine-degree water, but officials told him that, even so, he had to complete the race to collect the prize money. Enraged, Lumsdon swam on, while Canadians telephoned every radio and television station and newspaper in Toronto with pledges of

money, goods, and even a hunting lodge for Lumsdon, whether he finished or not. After nineteen hours and forty-two minutes in the water, Lumsdon staggered on shore in front of a screaming crowd. He had won eighty-four thousand dollars, the hunting lodge, and the adoration of every Canadian.

Lake Michigan Marathons

The sight of thirty-five thousand Canadians sitting in the grandstands in Toronto, watching a swimmer for hours on a freezing day, gave Chicago businessman Jim Moran an idea. Already a whiz at selling cars—in the late 1950s Moran's Courtesy Ford dealership was the biggest in the country, and he had pioneered car ads on

JIM DREYER: MASTER OF THE GREAT LAKES

To swim across one Great Lake is an extraordinary feat. Jim Dreyer has crossed them all but Lake Superior. Since 1998, Dreyer, a Michigan businessman in his thirties, has braved excruciatingly cold water (rarely above fifty-five degrees), high winds, bad weather, and enormous distances in pursuit of his quest. Even more amazing is the fact that until 1995 Dreyer was a water-phobic nonswimmer.

Each of his routes across the Lakes has been more than fifty miles, and during these swims, which have taken at least thirty-nine hours to complete, Dreyer spends at least one night in the water while his escort boat lights his way. However, during his Lake Huron swim, four miles away from the Canadian shore, the boat designated to escort Dreyer and his two support swimmers failed to show up. They swam the remaining four miles in darkness, using a lighthouse to guide them.

In July 2000 Dreyer set himself a three-day triathlon—he would swim Lake Erie, run a marathon, bike to the south shore of Lake Ontario, and swim across to Toronto. However, severe dehydration after running the marathon forced him to stop; after recovering, Dreyer completed the event that August.

Only Superior, the largest, coldest Great Lake, remains unconquered. Three attempts were thwarted by hypothermia and high waves, and in all three tries, Dreyer swam for more than forty hours. "I won't be sure this feat is humanly possible until I do it," Dreyer wrote on his website (www.swimjimswim.com) before his first Superior swim. "But I do believe that if it is possible, I'm the human who can do it."

How does Dreyer make these "impossible" swims? "The human body is infinitely adaptable, but it does have limits," he says. "But the human spirit knows no limitations, especially when driven by a force larger than ourselves. For me that force is the Big Brothers/Big Sisters program." Each of Dreyer's swims has raised money for that organization. He says, "[It's] my mission to remind people that our children are waiting . . . for a real hero to come into their lives and bring a brighter future."

TV—he was also a tireless fund-raiser for charity. Unlike many businessmen of his time, Moran was an exercise buff—specifically a swimmer. A Great Lake lay in his front yard. An open water marathon in Chicago seemed natural.

The first Lake Michigan Challenge was held on August 21, 1961. Six swimmers, three men and three women, left from the seawall on Chicago's waterfront at 8:00

A.M. headed for Michigan City, Indiana. Eighteen hours later, only one, Ted Erikson, was left. But in darkness and bad weather, Erikson and his boat crew had gone more than 13 miles off course. This made the swim a distance of 44 miles instead of 36.75. Erikson finally reached the pier in Michigan City at 8:37 P.M. on August 22 after swimming for thirty-six hours and thirty-seven minutes in high wind and waves. The first person to swim across Lake Michigan, Erikson swam more than twice the distance of either the English or Catalina Channel swims and even put the feats of many Lake Ontario swimmers in the shade. Moran reaped more publicity from newspapers, radio, and television in the Midwest than he could possibly pay for, and he was planning the next year's race within a week.

The 1962 race was set along the western edge of Lake Michigan from Chicago to Waukegan, Illinois, thirty-six miles to the north. As an added attraction, Moran promised ten thousand dollars to the swimmer who could reach Kenosha, Wisconsin, a race distance of fifty miles from Chicago. The prize money lured Danish open water champion Greta Anderson, but she was five minutes behind winner Dennis Matuch when they reached Waukegan twenty-one hours after leaving Chicago. Matuch took the four-thousand-dollar prize for reaching Waukegan, and quit. He was the first man ever to beat Anderson in a race. But since the only way she would win any money at all was to go on to Kenosha, Anderson, pursued by the now famous Erikson, kept on. It took Anderson ten hours to cover the remaining fourteen miles, but at the end, she set a new record for open water swimming—fifty miles in thirty-one hours.

The next year's race pushed the distance, and the competitors, even further.

The distance, at sixty miles from Chicago to Benton Harbor-Saint Joseph, Michigan, would set a new record. The prize was fifteen thousand dollars, at the time the third largest for any swimming event in history. Greta Anderson returned, but the prize contestant was the legendary Egyptian marathoner, Abo-Heif.

On August 17, 1963, Abo-Heif had won the CNE race, taking the lead at the thirteen-mile mark and sprinting through

Among the top swimmers of 1962, Greta Anderson swam a record fifty miles in thirty-one hours.

the fifty-five-degree water to set a new record in the Lake Ontario swims. On August 21 he emerged from Lake Michigan, thirty-four hours and thirty-eight minutes after leaving Chicago. Abo-Heif, a thirty-four-year-old army officer and an accomplished classical pianist who spoke six languages, was the undisputed world champion of professional open water swimming, a title he held through the 1960s. Meanwhile, Jim Moran called it

quits as a race promoter. Rising costs had made swimming marathons less attractive from a financial standpoint, but in the six years he had sponsored Lake Michigan swims, he had helped change the history of marathon swimming.

Recent History

In the 1970s and early 1980s, long-distance and open water swimming competition fell into relative obscurity in the United States

---

STRAIT SISTERS: LYNNE COX AND MIMI HUGHES

The Bering Strait is only 2.7 miles wide. But the water between Little Diomede Island, Alaska, and Big Diomede Island, Russia, is about thirty-seven degrees Fahrenheit—when it is not frozen solid. When Lynne Cox first thought of swimming across the Strait in the early 1980s, that narrow strip of cold water separated the world's two superpower antagonists, the Soviet Union and the United States. That is what attracted Cox, one of the world's best cold water marathon swimmers. "In my life, I try to make connections," she says. "The core of what I do is to try to impact the world in a positive way."

Cox swam the Strait in 1987. Despite the cold, she made the two-hour-and-six-minute trip in a standard swimsuit, goggles, and cap. "The swim itself turned out to be the easiest part," she said in the Spring 1996 issue of *Rodale's Fitness Swimmer* magazine. "It was cold, but I didn't have any problems until I got to the Soviet side and found out that the people waiting for me were about half mile down the beach. So I swam down to meet them."

Cox reached both her goals—the swim and the connections. "She proved by her courage how closely to each other our people live," said Russian president Mikhail Gorbachev in the same magazine article. He signed a missile-reduction treaty later that year, a big step in ending the Cold War with the United States.

Ten years later, in 1997, the world had changed but the Bering Strait had not. It attracted Mimi Hughes, a Tennessee teacher and mother, who brought along "tons of expensive technical gadgets" to help pick the best time to swim. "But in the end, I relied on the knowledge of the local residents," she says. "They made me wait two days, then one morning they said, 'Go now' so I did." Three hours later, Hughes shook hands on the other side with a Russian pen pal whom she had never met. "Afterward, it was hard to believe it really happened," Hughes said in a 1999 telephone interview. "But I know now that there's nothing in life I can't handle."

and Canada, though it continued to be popular in the rest of the world. Since about 1985, however, many amateur open water races have been organized, often in the context of triathlons. This has revived interest in North America in the whole field of open water swimming.

There are two classes of races, based on distance. Open water swims are 1.5 kilometers (about a mile) to 25 kilometers, (about 15.5 miles). Any race longer than 25 kilometers, or which lasts more than five hours, is a marathon. There are several sanctioning organizations for races: The World Professional Marathon Swim Federation (WPMSF), founded in 1963, is based in Fort Lauderdale, Florida, while the Federation Internationale de Natation de Longue Distance has been based since 1954 in Heliopolis, Egypt, which is the site of the annual Marathon of the Nile. FINA, the international sanctioning body for all of swimming, set up a World Cup championship in 1997 that operates under WPMSF rules.

Though most North Americans still do not know of professional marathon swimming, amateur open water swimming is the fastest growing kind of swim competition around the world. There are dozens of open water swims in the United States and Canada which attract large fields of elite amateur swimmers. Many races are simply for fun or to raise money for a charity, but some of them are so prestigious that serious recreational swimmers who qualify to compete in them can find themselves swimming against (or probably in the wakes of) some world-class racers. Unlike most sports, open water racing affords the chance for a fan to compete with the top people in the sport, one of the biggest reasons why it is likely to continue to grow in popularity among swimmers.

CHAPTER 3

Women Jump into Swimming

While swimming was developing in the nineteenth century into the modern sport we know today, women were noticeably absent. Victorian standards of behavior for women kept them swathed in multiple layers of clothing; physical exertion was considered unladylike, and in any case, was impossible for women who were bound into corsets so tight the wearer could barely breathe. No respectable woman in Europe, North America, or Australia would show any part of her body in public other than her face and hands, so women had separate public baths, pools, and even beaches.

The spectators at the earliest swimming competitions were entirely men, for two reasons: One, until the mid-to-late nineteenth century, men swam naked, and two, swimming races were held expressly for the purpose of gambling on them, another activity from which women were barred.

However, by the end of the nineteenth century, many doctors were promoting swimming for women for both health and hygiene. Several women's swimming associations were formed in Britain and Europe. Women's swimming became part of the Olympics in 1912 when a 100-meter freestyle race, a 4x100 freestyle relay, and a diving event for females were added to the Stockholm Games.

Until the late twentieth century, most speed swimming champions were teenage girls whose competitive careers were over before they were old enough to vote. This was partly because of the mistaken belief that female athletic performance peaked in the teens, and partly due to a lack of opportunity for young women to pursue sports after high school or college. However, in the past twenty-five years, shifts in social attitudes toward women's sports, and more athletic opportunities for females, have prolonged the time at the top for many women swimmers. This longevity has allowed swimmers to mature, physically and mentally; coupled with new methods of coaching, it has resulted in steadily lowered women's times in every competitive event.

Women Get in the Water

While swimming had a decidedly male outlook until at least the late nineteenth century, there were women swimmers and even some racers. Early women swimmers (who were often feminists), such as Australia's Annette Kellerman, railed against both the double standards of dress and behavior for men and women and the perception of women as frail, fragile creatures incapable of handling any demands on their bodies.

Kellerman and other women swimmers were not above using ideals of femininity to promote swimming for women. "When

Women venture into the sea at Brighton, England, in 1825. Western social etiquette at this time demanded women be clad in "bathing dresses" to enter the water.

THE EVOLUTION OF WOMEN'S SWIMSUITS

To us, the "bathing dress" worn by women one hundred years ago looks ridiculous—and downright dangerous. Weighted down by yards of wet fabric, how could a woman hope to swim? In 1900 a male swimming teacher named Gundula Wolters attempted to swim in a woman's suit. He was appalled. Wolters, as quoted in the *International Encyclopedia of Women and Sports*, wrote later, "In that gear a swim of 100 yards was as serious a task as a mile in my own suit. . . . I no longer wondered why so few women swim well, but rather that they are able to swim at all."

In 1915, *Silk*, a silk industry trade publication, described a one-piece silk swimming suit which incorporated a dress and knee-length pants as "a very fetching garment, especially when it is completed with the proper shoes, stockings and cap, and adorned with a bunch of rubber flow-

ers." No matter that Fanny Durack competed in the 1912 Olympics in a short tank suit or that Annette Kellerman showed off her skills in a neck-to-ankles, form-fitting black silk knit suit—"respectable" women still went in the water fully clad.

Within ten years, women and men both sported tank suits—scoop-necked tops with shoulder straps and shorts that reached to mid- or upper thigh. Women's suits shortened to cover just the torso by the mid-1920s, though men and boys could not bare their chests until the 1940s.

"Racing" suits introduced the stretch fabric Lycra to swimmers in the mid-1960s, and through the 1970s and 1980s, competition suits got lighter—and skimpier. For the 2000 season, swimsuits went back to covering most of a racer's body—though in a way that was much more revealing than one hundred years ago.

we consider the element of grace in swimming, as well as the mere exhibition of strength, we must concede that women outrank men as swimmers," she wrote in 1918.[7] Swimming was seen by the more open-minded segment of the male population as an ideal women's sport—graceful, restrained, and less sweaty than other sports. Swimming was promoted as an ideal way for women to become better mothers—the idea was that they would be accustomed to water and bathing for cleanliness and would develop the discipline to devote their lives to their families.

The First Young Champions

Some women, however, had different ideas. Partly inspired by women swimmers competing in the 1912 Games, Charlotte Epstein founded the National Women's Lifesaving League in New York in 1914. Apart from teaching women how to rescue and resuscitate people from drowning, the league was intended to give women a place to learn to swim and compete. Epstein persuaded the Amateur Athletic Union to allow women swimmers to register as athletes, and in 1917 she started the New York Women's Swimming

Association (NYWSA). This became the first American women's swimming team.

Epstein's cofounder of the NYWSA was Louis de Breda Handley, who was a volunteer coach of the New York Athletic Club. Epstein and Handley produced virtually all the female swimmers and divers the United States sent to the Olympics in 1920, 1924, and 1928, starting with Ethelda Bleibtrey. In August 1919 Bleibtrey set a world record (6 minutes, 30.2 seconds) in the 440-yard freestyle event at the Amateur Athletic Union championships. At the Antwerp Games in 1920, she became the first American woman to win a gold medal in the Olympics, setting a new world record (1:13.6) in the 100-meter freestyle. Bleibtrey collected her second gold with another record-breaking swim in the 300 freestyle, and a third when she set a new record in the 400 freestyle relay. In all, the women of the NYWSA took every medal available to women in swimming and diving competitions at that Olympics. Their success opened the way for women's track and field events in the

Ethelda Bleibtrey (right) and her teammates pose after practice. Bleibtrey was the first female athlete sponsored by the NYWSA to swim in the Olympics.

1924 Games and the subsequent development of many women's Olympic events.

Bleibtrey and her teammates set another precedent in women's swimming—they were all very young. Bleibtrey was eighteen, diver Helen Wainwright was fifteen, and swimmer/diver Aileen Riggin, who became the youngest gold medalist at Antwerp, was all of fourteen. "The U.S. Olympic Committee didn't want to take children to the Olympics," a ninety-six-year-old Riggin (deceased December 2002) remembered. "They asked who would take care of us. But our club manager, Charlotte Epstein, and our coach, Mr. Handley, went down there and said, 'What are you doing to these kids who worked so hard?' And we wound up going."[8]

The fact that these early champions were young is not surprising. In those days amateur swimming was strictly amateur. A swimmer could lose his or her nonprofessional standing by taking a job related to swimming, such as life guarding. Athletic scholarships, especially for girls, were many years in the future. Even women's college swim teams were a few years off. Only girls from wealthy or middle-class families that could support them while they swam were able to spend time training. Once these world champions reached their early twenties, it was expected that even they would marry and start families, and their racing careers would be over.

The Queen of the Channel

Another very young champion who came out of the Women's Swimming Association (WSA) was Gertrude Ederle. She joined the WSA in 1918 at the age of twelve and became the all-time youngest female to hold a swimming record. At sixteen she set an open water record for 3.5 miles (1:1:34) while beating a predominantly male field in the Manhattan Beach to Brighton Beach swim. Like many of her contemporaries, Ederle was a great all-around swimmer, capable of winning both long- and short-distance races, either indoors or outdoors, in a pool or in open water. When her amateur career ended after the 1924 Olympics, Ederle had won 250 races, set nine new world records, won bronze medals for the 100- and 400-meter freestyle, and earned a gold for the freestyle relay.

The following year Ederle turned professional and set out to conquer the English Channel. Her first attempt failed after nine hours, but on August 6, 1926, Ederle not only made it from France to England, but set a new record (14:31) in the process. As a women's record, Ederle's time held until 1950.

Only three weeks later, the second woman swam the Channel. Mille Gade Corson, the mother of two, was twenty-seven. It took her an hour longer than Ederle to make the swim, but much ado was made in the press about her age and motherhood. Corson's kids were the reason for her swim, she said;

Gertrude Ederle trains for her cross-channel swim in 1925.

she hoped she could earn enough money from it for their education.

Meanwhile, when Ederle returned to the United States in October, she was greeted with acclaim. A ticker tape parade down Broadway, a personal note from the president of the United States, and national and international fame were her recognition for crossing the Channel, but she had accomplished more than that.

By becoming the first woman to set a sporting record that established a standard for *both* genders, Ederle convincingly smashed the foundations of the idea that women were inferior to men. She demonstrated that women could develop their physical, emotional, and psychological strength to perform at their peak just as well as men could. Most significantly for the sport of swimming, she also established that the crawl, paired with a six- or eight-beat kick, was the most efficient way to swim.

At the age of nineteen, Ederle reached the peak of her swimming career. She had no more goals to attain. She turned down an invitation to participate in the first Catalina Channel race and spent a few years swimming in exhibitions and vaudeville. She made one movie and retired from swimming in 1928. In the late 1930s, the showman Billy Rose persuaded her to appear in his famous Aquacade, a water spectacle. After that, Ederle turned her attention to teaching deaf children, which she did until retirement. Except for acting as an advisor to a YMCA swimming program in New York City, she had no further activity in the sport.

American Women at the Olympics

Women continued to occupy a prominent place in open water swimming, but Americans proved to be far more interested in speed swimming than in marathons. Many elite women's colleges started aquatics programs, and YMCA programs opened swim competition to both boys and girls.

In the Olympics, the American women continued their domination of freestyle through the 1932 Los Angeles Games, though English, Dutch, and German female swimmers took medals in the backstroke and breaststroke events that had been added. At the 1936 Berlin Olympics, the Dutch women's team surged to the fore, taking all but one medal; Willie van Ouden's 100-meter freestyle record (1:04.6) stood for twenty years, the longest-held record for either sex in swimming history.

Hungarian swimmers took most of the women's events in the 1952 Games, while in 1956, Australians Dawn Fraser and Lorraine Crapp broke several records. The 1956 Games saw the addition of both the men's 200-meter and women's 100-meter butterfly events. After 1956, changes slowly made the women's programs more similar to the men's: 4x100 and 4x400 medley relays were added in 1960, and the 200-meter backstroke, the 200 butterfly, the 100 breaststroke, and the 200 individual medley in 1968. With the addition of the 4x200 freestyle relay in 1996, the only difference now between men's and women's Olympic swimming events is the distance races—men still go fifteen hundred meters, and women eight hundred.

American women regained their dominance in the 1960s (though Australian Fraser became the first woman to break one minute in the 100-meter in 1964) with record-setting swims by Debbie Meyers, Kathy Ferguson, Sharon Stouder, and Donna De Varona. In particular, American women were the masters of the 4x100 freestyle relay. They won gold medals at every Olympics from 1960 to 1984, except in 1980, the year the United States boycotted the Moscow Olympics to protest the invasion of Afghanistan by the Soviet Union. American women reasserted control in 1992 in Barcelona, setting a world record of 3:39.46 seconds, won again in Atlanta, and set another world record at Sydney with a time of 3:36.61. That 1992 relay team was notable for the fact that three of the swimmers—Dara Torres, Jenny Thompson, and Amy Van Dyken—had swum the 4x100 freestyle relay at least once before, and Torres had done it four times. Thompson and Van Dyken were both in their late twenties, and Torres, at thirty-four, was the oldest-ever member of a U.S. Olympic swimming team. Collectively, they had aged the face of the female swimming champion more than twenty years.

Champions Get "Older"

The widespread notion that top female athletes had to be in their teens or early twenties had no scientific basis. People—including swimmers—just assumed that

AGE IS NO OBJECT

Though female swimming champions in their mid-twenties had become commonplace and she had medals from three previous Olympics, Dara Torres's decision to train for the 2000 U.S. Olympic squad was met with skepticism. At thirty-three, she had not swum a lap in seven years.

Undaunted, Torres moved to Palo Alto, California, to train with Richard Quick, head coach at Stanford University, and the coach of the U.S. Olympic women's swim team. A year of essentially relearning how to swim followed, but Torres's talent and competitive fire quickly resurfaced. She trained long and hard every day in the pool and in the weight room. She adopted a new diet and added pounds of muscle. In the preliminaries to the 2000 Olympics, she set new American records in the 50-meter freestyle (25.29 seconds) and the 100 butterfly (57.58).

At Sydney, her triumph was complete. Torres won five medals: gold in the freestyle relay, gold in the medley relay (which set a new world record of 3:58.30), and bronze medals in the 100 butterfly, the 100 freestyle, and the 50 freestyle. At

Dara Torres breaks the surface of the water during the women's 100-meter butterfly at the 2000 Olympics.

the age of thirty-four, she became not only the oldest-ever member of a U.S. Olympic swim team, but the only swimmer to win medals in four Olympics.

Torres bolstered the contention that female athletes peak in their thirties rather than their teens. As she matured, her times in the 50 freestyle dropped: Her time at age thirty-four—24.63—is nearly a full second faster than the 25.61 she set at age eighteen. No longer can elite level swimming be considered exclusive to high school- and college-age athletes. Torres has shown that women can compete at the highest levels of swimming into their thirties.

athletic performance naturally began to decline in the twenties. With fewer professional athletic options than men, most women expected that their competitive careers would end with college graduation. In general, organized sports competition for postcollege women, either amateur or professional, was extremely limited until the last quarter of the twentieth century.

Several factors helped broaden the opportunities for women. One was that many members of the Baby Boom generation embraced the idea that exercise needed to be a permanent part of a healthy life. The Boomers' yearning for eternal youth led to the creation of "Masters" programs—teams and competition for adults—in many sports. U.S. Masters Swimming was among the first, beginning in 1972. A combination of more leisure time and more media coverage of sports led to greater interest in competitions of all sorts. Increased coverage offered more advertising possibilities for businesses, and

AGING-UP AND SWIMMING FASTER: KARLYN PIPES-NEILSEN

In the spring of 2002, Karlyn Pipes-Neilsen became the first woman over forty to break the one-minute barrier in both the 100-meter freestyle (lowering a record she had set only a month before) and the 100-yard individual medley.

Then she proceeded to smash eight more U.S. Masters records, which would have been world records if they had been set in a FINA-sanctioned meet. But for Pipes-Neilsen, it was just another day at the races; she has been at the top of the highly competitive U.S. Masters women's 30–34 and 35–39 age-groups since returning to swimming in 1993.

Pipes-Neilsen is testament to the athletic power and potential of women in their thirties. She swam competitively in her teens and for a year in college before quitting both school and swimming. Coming back to both at thirty-two, she became the oldest female swimmer to set several NCAA Division II records. After graduation she entered Masters competition. In the past nine years she has set fifty world records; fifteen of them (and twenty-six U.S. records) since she "aged-up" in March 2002. (Masters swimmers compete in age-groups in five-year increments; they do not get older, they "age up.")

"I'm still setting some 'lifetime bests', though not as often as I used to," Pipes-Neilsen said in an interview in November 2002. "And my current times in some events ... are faster than I did when I was younger."

"I don't think I'm unique—the level of competition in my age group is very stiff. We are the fastest women in Masters. I think female swimmers my age, who graduated from high school at the very beginning of Title IX, didn't have the chance to develop their full potential in college swimming. We got frustrated and gave it up, then when we got older we decided to find out how good we really could be."

thus, more sponsorship. In turn, that led to more professional opportunities for athletes of all kinds—and both genders. Sponsorship allows more women to keep pursuing their athletic careers after college.

Along with this explosion of interest in sports came Title IX, the federal regulation which requires all colleges and universities that receive federal funds to give equal athletic opportunities to males and females. This increased the number of swimming scholarships available to young women, allowing more females to train intensively with top coaches.

Together, these changes have made it easier for women to excel as swimmers. Now women swimmers have the opportunity to show they can drastically improve their abilities into their late twenties, and during the past decade, they have regularly turned in new peak performances.

These shifting social attitudes toward women in sports allow women to fully exploit their physical potential, believes Joel Stager, a professor of exercise physiology at Indiana University. He has been tracking men's and women's swimming performance for several years and has concluded that women have a better chance of reaching their peak at a later age, probably even later than men do. (Male speed swimming champions are still virtually all under twenty-five.) "Peak performance means being at the limits of your inherent capabilities," says Stager. "A lot of things

factor into that—optimal conditioning, optimal nutrition, optimal physical and mental health." Now that women can remain in training into their late twenties and early thirties, they have a better chance of finding their ultimate levels. "The top swimmers in the world expect peak performance only once every several years," he says. "But we are seeing them now whenever women compete at the championship level."

Changes in social attitudes have also redesigned the female athlete, continues Stager. The attitude toward weight training has shifted, and Stager says, "Through time in the weight room, many . . . female athletes have developed bodies that the public perceives as something to strive for instead of to be ashamed of. We've dropped the moniker of 'tomboy' from our vocabulary."[9]

Still, Stager and other researchers are just beginning to investigate the physical factors that appear to prolong top athletic performance in women. Though the numbers—constantly dropping records—are evidence that women swimmers do get better as they get older, scientists are still trying to find out why, and whether or not there are physical differences between men and women that may cause them to peak as athletes at different ages.

Meanwhile, many women who compete in Masters swimming are also finding themselves going faster as they get older and,

Scientists are still researching why many women athletes reach their physical peak in their thirties and forties.

in many cases, beating their college times when they are in their thirties and even forties. For instance, Nancy Rideout, a college swimmer, joined the newly founded U.S. Masters at age thirty. It took her four years to break the minute mark in the 100-meter freestyle, a feat she had never done in school. Ten years later, she had her time down to 58.2, and now she holds several Masters 50–54 age-group records. "I had dreams and goals for my swimming in my teens," she says, "but I figured they were down the tubes after school. I finally reached those in my 40s. My swimming went downhill in my early 50s, so I changed my training. My swimming career turned about 180 degrees, and the times I achieved at age 54 were as personally rewarding and satisfying to me as any others."[10]

A Look at the Record Book

Many experts believe that women's swimming is the most competitive it has ever been. Records fall regularly in every type of swimming in each age-group from USA Swimming kids' teams through college teams and into Masters. The women's

50-meter freestyle Olympic time dropped over 1.1 seconds between 1988 and 2000, from 25.49 to 24.13 set by twenty-seven-year-old Inge de Bruijn. At the Sydney Games in 2000, Misty Hyman was a full five seconds faster winning gold in the 200-meter butterfly than Li Lin had been when setting a world record at Barcelona eight years before. Though there are too many variables to make valid comparisons of men's and women's records, in general, women's fastest times now match those set by men between the mid-1960s and early 1970s. Overall, women's records are reset more frequently than men's, probably due to the combination of improved training and longer competitive careers for women. Unfortunately, the suspicion that illegal drug use also plays a role still looms over women's swimming.

CHAPTER 4

Doping: Swimming's Biggest Scandal

For a long time, swimming avoided the issue of performance-enhancing drugs and other illegal substances because the only ergogenic (performance-boosting) aids available, stimulants and anabolic steroids, were not beneficial to swimmers. But swimming authorities could no longer ignore doping, as illegal drug use is known, after the early 1990s, when the extent to which it had been practiced by some national swimming teams became public.

Amphetamines and other "energizers" were never widely used by swimmers, because they are unreliable as performance-enhancers and easily detected in urine tests. Over the years, a few swimmers fell afoul of drug tests for stimulants by inadvertently taking nonprescription drugs such as cold remedies and decongestants or prescribed asthma medications that contained the banned stimulants. Anabolic steroids, synthetic compounds that increase muscle bulk, had little attraction to swimmers at first. While big muscles are valuable to body builders and football players, they are actually a burden in the pool; in swimming, speed comes more from good technique than from muscle power. So taking a muscle-building drug just did not pay off for swimmers.

Swimming became vulnerable to the problem of doping when ergogenic aids became more sophisticated. Now drugs can speed muscle recovery, boost oxygen absorption, and reduce lactic acid buildup—

SYNTHETIC OR NATURAL, STEROIDS ARE BANNED

Steroids occur naturally in the human body, where they play a host of roles relating to cell growth. Anabolic tissue building steroids are synthetic compounds which speed up that process in part by raising the body's level of testosterone, the male hormone. They build more muscle fiber, faster, than the body does normally. It is said that women who take steroids build 40 percent more muscle than women who do not.

But the problem with steroids is that the human body—male or female—reacts badly in many ways to large doses. Along with big muscles, many steroid users develop severe acne, lose their hair, and become irritable, short-tempered, and aggressive. Children who take steroids before they are finished growing may never reach their full natural height. Many of the German women who were forced to take steroids while they were Olympic athletes in the 1970s and 1980s have had a host of serious health prob-

The press spokesman for German Customs displays a seized shipment of anabolic steroids.

lems in their adult years. Many have either had trouble conceiving babies or borne children with birth defects. Others have had heart and liver diseases uncommon in young adults.

When the dangers of synthetic steroids became known, athletes and sports scientists began to look for other, more naturally occuring forms of male hormones.

But "natural anabolics" such as androstenedione, though they can be derived from beef and are legal food supplements, are also banned by most sports authorities. In part, this is because the effects and potential side effects of such substances are unknown, and also because taking these kinds of performance boosters is considered cheating.

SHIRLEY BABASHOFF: BEATEN BY CHEATING

Shirley Babashoff joined the legendary Mission Viejo Nadadores, a Southern California swim club, at age eight. Shirley was fifteen when she won two silver medals at the 1972 Munich Games, as well as a gold for the women's 4x100 freestyle relay. By the age of seventeen, she had mastered distance events as well as sprints, taking medals in every event from the 100-meter to the 800. In recognition, the U.S. Olympic Committee named her Sportswoman of the Year in 1974.

At the U.S. Olympic Trials for the 1976 Games in Montreal, Shirley set a world record in the 800 freestyle. Favored to win again at multiple distances and in the individual medley, she came second in every event (except the freestyle relay) to the suddenly dominant East Germans. The GDR team not only won by unprecedented margins, but they performed unlikely feats, such as Kornelia Ender's two gold medals in events less than thirty minutes apart.

Babashoff was not shy about expressing her opinions. She said publicly that she believed the Germans were cheating (though they passed all the drug tests), and was dubbed "Surly Shirley" by the press, which considered her nothing more than a sore loser. Even some other coaches considered that the American women could not handle losing.

After Montreal Shirley enrolled in UCLA, where she swam for a year, but her experience at the 1976 Olympics had soured her on swimming. Today, many swimmers and coaches believe she could possibly have won five gold medals in 1976 if the competition had been clean and fair. This would have put her among the greatest swimmers in the world.

all of which can allow a swimmer to train harder and longer with less recovery time between practices. This has made doping more alluring to some swimmers, who are willing to risk their reputations, careers, and health to win. No one knows how pervasive drug use is, though most American observers say that frequent random testing at the elite level, combined with antidrug education programs, appears to have controlled the problem in the sport in the United States.

Unfortunately, swimming did not confront this problem until it became apparent that there was widespread drug use in the national swimming programs of China, the former Soviet Union, and the German Democratic Republic. Neither FINA nor the International Olympic Committee (IOC) implemented intensive drug-testing programs until after the medical directors and coaches of the national sports teams from the former East Germany were put on trial for systematically giving very young athletes illegal drugs. Now elite swimmers are subjected to frequent, unannounced, out-of-competition testing. Even though only a few fail the tests, the cloud of suspicion still hangs over every swim meet.

Turning Drugs into Gold

"It was pretty obvious at the time that the East German women's swim team was cheating," remembers Ray Essick, retired executive director of USA Swimming. "There just wasn't any way then, in the 1970s, to prove it, but you could tell just by looking at them."[11] The women, most of them teenagers, were unusually large and heavily muscled, with broad shoulders and flat chests and hips. If their appearance was somewhat masculine, their voices certainly were; one American swimmer is said to have fled to her coach in a panic, saying there were men in the women's locker room. It was the East German women.

The German Democractic Republic (GDR), or Communist East Germany, had committed itself to dominating all types of international sports competition. This was supposed to show the world the superiority of its socialist political and economic system. In some sports, this worked, but the GDR had never done well in swimming— no wins, no medals—until 1973.

That year, the GDR women dominated the world swimming championship in Belgrade, and between then and the 1976 Montreal Olympics, they reset virtually every world record. At Montreal, the East German women took eleven of the thirteen gold medals and set seven world records. They continued their dominance through the 1970s, and then swam virtually unopposed at the 1980 Moscow Olympics. (In fact, the GDR's athletes won 75 percent of *all* the medals awarded at the 1980 Games.) When the East Germans (and the rest of the Soviet bloc teams) were absent from the 1984 Los Angeles Olympics, the United States briefly regained dominance, but the GDR women came back at the 1988 Seoul Games.

The media, coaches, and athletes said openly at the time that they believed the GDR athletes were using steroids and other performance-enhancing drugs. Because drug testing did not turn up any evidence against them, the accusations were never made official. In addition, when swimmers who had lost to the East Germans complained about the cheating, they were often labeled sore losers. The East Germans steadfastly maintained that their unique system of identifying promising athletes early and setting them to intensive, innovative training regimes from childhood was producing the records. Many observers thought excellent and innovative training was the reason for the GDR's athletic success.

Then, in 1989, the Berlin Wall was torn down, and the Communist government of the GDR collapsed with it. Germany was quickly reunified, and many East Germans began to come forward with stories of how they had been victimized by the Stasi, the Communist regime's secret police. Among them were many athletes, including record setters and swimming-medal winners like Petra Schneider and Christine Knacke-Sommer.

They told horrifying stories of being forced to take steroid and male hormone shots from the ages of thirteen or fourteen. They recounted being warned to wear long-sleeved shirts as much as possible to hide the needle marks. In many cases, girls as young as ten or eleven were given what they were told were vitamin pills, but which in reality were steroids. "They didn't treat us like humans," Jutta Klas said on ABC's *20-20* in 2000. "We were treated like machines." Klas believes her daughter's blindness is due to the drugs she herself was forced to take as a young swimmer.[12]

The Stasi's files were opened and confirmed the stories—the athletic authorities of the GDR, obeying direct orders from the government, had been cheating on a massive scale, in all sports and all kinds of international competition, since at least the late 1960s.

Between March 1998 and July 2000 a series of trials in Germany convicted most of the directors and doctors for the former GDR swim team of illegally doping their athletes. However, the fines that were levied were small, and all the jail sentences suspended. Several of the East German athletes who had testified against their former coaches and doctors voluntarily surrendered their medals.

The realization that neither FINA nor the IOC had been able to detect a single instance of illegal drug use by the East Germans over nearly twenty years did severe damage to both organizations' credibility on drug use and drug testing. Even though it is now known that virtually every East German athlete, either knowingly or innocently, had been on illegal drugs when they were setting records and winning medals, neither FINA nor the IOC has moved to rescind those awards. Many athletes and national teams have protested that they were unfairly robbed of victories and records.

China's Sudden Success

Just as the East German women had done in the 1970s, the Chinese women's swimming team made a sudden huge splash in international competition in the 1990s. From being unable to make it past preliminary heats in most meets in the 1980s, Chinese women began sweeping medals and records in 1991. Finally, at the 1994 World Championships in Rome, where they won twelve of the sixteen gold medals available, the simmering anger and suspicions of swimmers and coaches of other nations boiled over.

Led by Dave Johnson, the head coach of the Canadian team, representatives from eighteen countries demanded that FINA start a more rigorous system of drug testing. By that fall, a more sophisticated test had discovered that the Chinese swimmers were using a newly discovered form of testosterone, which they administered via a skin massage cream. Moreover, they were caught because the drug tests were taken immediately after they stepped off a long plane trip, and before they could take the diuretic (water) pills that would have flushed the traces of the drug out of their systems.

Faced with eleven positive drug tests, the Chinese swimming authorities dropped the defense that their swimmers were just strong, hardworking peasant girls who used traditional Chinese herbal remedies. They admitted that several coaches and swimmers were doping in hopes of collecting prize money. Three visits from FINA delegations, in 1995, 1998, and 1999, yielded mixed results on Chinese control of drug use. In 1999 three Chinese swimmers and five trainers en route to the World Cup meet in Sydney were intercepted by Australian authorities and deported when they were discovered carrying illegal drugs; the following year, more Chinese athletes and trainers were again caught with drugs on their way to the Olympics. That year the Chinese women swimmers won no medals at the Olympics.

Suspicions persist about the Chinese women swimmers. "They have very unpredictable results," says American breaststroke gold medalist Megan Quann. "Someone will have one spectacular time at a meet, then you'll never hear of her again. They do great at one meet, and terribly at the next. The top Chinese women tend to swim at only a few meets a year, so you have to wonder what they're doing the rest of the time." [13]

Queens of the Lanes Dethroned

Many observers believe that the majority of elite swimmers are drug free. As evidence, they point to the very few positive tests that turn up in the many hundreds which are administered to elite swimmers every year. However, two highly visible female swimmers have been punished for drug use in recent years.

Irish swimmer Michelle Smith's performance went from mediocre to spectacular after her 1994 marriage to her personal coach, Dutch shot-putter Erik de Bruin. Since her husband had been banned from competition in the early 1990s for excess levels of testosterone in his blood, many observers assumed that Smith's improvement came from doping. Her defenders said the sudden drop in her times in events such as the 400-meter individual medley was just the natural result of settling down, maturing, gaining experience, and having a great coach. But winning three gold medals at the 1996 Olympics stepped up the suspicions about her, even though none of Smith's times were records. Repeated postcompetition and out-of-competition testing of Smith was negative, but in 1998 a surprise urine test was found to contain a lethal level of alcohol. This led to suspicions that Smith, by this time going by her married name, de Bruin, had tampered with the sample to disguise traces of illegal drugs.

In August 1998, de Bruin was banned by FINA from international competition for four years. After losing an appeal in June 1999, de Bruin retired from swimming, still protesting her innocence.

A second Olympic gold medalist, Costa Rica's Claudia Poll, was banned from international competition for four years in June 2002 after testing positive for an illegal testosterone substance earlier in the year. Poll, who became her nation's only Olympic gold medalist when she won the 200-meter freestyle in Atlanta in 1996, immediately lodged a protest about the way the test was taken and appealed her suspension. She pointed out that she had tested clean fifty-five times previously, including eleven negative tests in 2001 and 2002. An appeal will be heard in 2003; until then, all Poll's results in any events which she swam during the six months prior to the test will be voided.

It should not be concluded from this that drug use is unique to female swimmers. Most certainly there have been and continue to be male swimmers who have also resorted to performance-enhancing drugs. The chief difference is that females who use male hormones and hormonelike substances such as anabolic steroids see

In a Swiss appeals court, Michelle de Bruin and her lawyer protest the Irish swimmer's four-year ban from international competition.

At the 2000 Summer Olympics, Megan Quann smiles during the medal presentation for the women's 100-meter breaststroke.

far greater results than males do and gain an even bigger edge over their competitors. "Women who use steroids can build 40 percent more muscle fiber than women who don't use them," points out Richard Quick, head coach of the Stanford University and U.S. Olympic women's teams. "Also, you become dramatically more aggressive. If you've got 10 meters to go in a race and you're tied with someone who doesn't use steroids, you've got a tremendous advantage because of the aggression that comes out."[14]

Clearly, women who take such drugs gain a far greater advantage over other women than men who dope gain over other men. So the benefit, at least in the short term, is far greater for women than it is for men. However, at the elite level in swimming, where the difference between winning and losing is often measured in hundredths of a second, males also can be lured by the promise of even a small improvement in performance. Given the enormous financial rewards that top swimmers can reap, it is not shocking that some athletes and their coaches abandon both their integrity and their good sense, and choose to use drugs.

Most top swimmers, though, do not use performance-boosting drugs. Megan Quann believes this is for a variety of reasons:

Apart from the fact that it's cheating, and that's wrong, I don't see how anyone can get any satisfaction out of winning if they know they're cheating. We work so hard, and that satisfaction is a big part of the reward. Besides, it can't be worth all the worrying that you're going to get caught. There are so many other things you can do to improve your swimming that are right and good—you don't have to use drugs to win. [15]

What Is Banned, and Why

There is a long list of drugs, both legal and illegal, which are banned for competition and training. All illegal drugs such as narcotics, hallucinogens, and stimulants such as methamphetamine are banned. Anabolic steroids and other prescription drugs like diuretics, local anesthetics, corticosteroids, and beta-blockers are also forbidden during training and competition. Performance-enhancing hormones such as testosterone and its derivatives are also forbidden, as are hormonelike compounds. Some legal stimulants such as pseudoephedrine (found in over-the-counter decongestants) and caffeine are allowed up to certain levels in training, but not in competition. Other herb-based stimulants such as ma huang and guarana, though classified as legal "foods" in some countries including the United States, are banned for athletes.

The latest focus of performance-enhancing substances appears to be on those which boost the oxygen-carrying capacity of the blood. Drugs like

CREATINE

In the past ten years, athletes looking for a legal performance booster and muscle builder have turned to creatine. Creatine is a substance found chiefly in meat, fish, and shellfish; muscle cells use it to burn energy from food. So creatine is not only crucial to athletic performance, but to life itself. The body also makes creatine, on its own, out of protein components called amino acids.

Many athletes have experimented with creatine to keep their energy level high and fatigue at bay, while others use it as a steroid substitute to build muscle in weight training. Since they burn more energy than the average person, athletes may need to consume more creatine in their diets, but that has not been determined. Many studies of athletes taking creatine indicate that it may help performance of sports which require brief, explosive bursts of action, such as the 50-meter freestyle. It does not appear to boost performance in sports that require longer, sustained effort, though, and at best, its performance-boosting powers are mild. There are many stories about its muscle-building capacities, but little scientific evidence to support them.

Creatine has been extensively tested in the past ten years and appears to be safe. However, some observers say using it is cheating, because it does have some ergogenic effect. It would be nearly impossible to test for it, though, since the body stores only a fixed amount, and excess is excreted. Therefore, enforcing a ban on creatine would be impossible. Others consider taking creatine on a par with taking vitamins—a sensible nutritional support for intense training, and nothing more.

erythropoietin are banned, as is the practice in which an athlete's blood is drawn, stored for a time until his or her body can generate replacement blood cells, then added back.

Since many of these drugs and practices cannot be detected in urine or can be concealed in various ways, FINA has tentatively approved some blood testing. Independent companies such as the private Norwegian consortium IDTM (the testers who snared Michelle Smith de Bruin) carry out analyses of athletes' blood down to the DNA structure. Unfortunately, more sophisticated testing is also much more expensive, which limits its use to only the athletes at the highest levels of the sport.

While some national swimming organizations, and some athletes, prefer testing be done by groups from their own countries, many more feel that only rigorously independent testing will dissipate the cloud of suspicion which still hangs over competitive swimming.

CHAPTER 5

Synchronized Swimming

For some, synchronized swimmers conjure up images of Hollywood bathing beauties in impossible fantasy movies with their color-coordinated costumes, waterproof stage makeup, and stylized moves. But in fact, synchronized swimming is an extraordinarily demanding sport, and the women—and the handful of men—who perform it are excellent athletes. Synchro swimming, as it is called, requires superb balance in the water, unusual breathing control, and intense body awareness.

It has been said about synchro swimmers that they do everything the dancer Ginger Rogers did (and Ginger did everything her partner Fred Astaire did, except she did it backward and in high heels),

except they do it upside down and underwater. That is a fair assessment of how difficult synchronized swimming is, but the origins of the sport owe more to ballet than to ballroom dancing. In fact, the sport we now know as synchronized swimming was called "water ballet" for many years.

From Stunts to Water Ballet

Some historians of women's sports describe synchronized swimming as the only sport invented by and for women. While it is true that the sport was developed and expanded by women, the first "stunt swimming" exhibitions were actually held by England's Royal Lifesaving Society (RLS), an all-male organization, in 1892. The "stunts" were similar to

BILL MAY: MALE SYNCHRO PIONEER

According to some sanctioning bodies like FINA and the IOC, Bill May does not even exist. That is because Bill May is something those groups do not recognize—a synchronized swimmer who happens to be male.

May, born in 1979 in upstate New York, has struggled past the negative attitudes about males in synchro since he took it up at age ten. He developed his talent well enough to be recruited by the Santa Clara (California) AquaMaids, a perennial national champion team, and moved there before he even finished high school. Currently, May is the U.S. national solo, duet, and figures champion, and a member of the U.S. champion team, Santa Clara, and the U.S. national team. He has won competitions in other countries which also have no rules against men in synchronized swimming, such

Bill May and his partner practice an underwater synchronized duet. May has always struggled with the gender bias in what is considered a sport for women.

as France and Switzerland. But FINA has so far resisted U.S. Synchro's attempts to create a mixed duet event in international competition, and as FINA goes, so go the Olympics. So May is barred from the ultimate challenge—and prize—in his sport. Still he hopes to persuade the IOC to include a mixed duet event as a demonstration sport at the 2004 Athens Olympics.

One problem is that he is the only American man competing at the elite level in the sport, and one of the handful in the world. FINA's stand is that they cannot alter synchro's women-only status until more men start competing. But without the Olympics as an ultimate goal, very few males will work so many years at such a demanding sport. The NCAA's rules against men in college synchro competition deter most would-be trailblazers also.

Bill May is likely to remain a standout in his sport for his gender as much as for his top-level talents.

figures synchronized swimmers must master today, says Dawn Pawson Bean, a former competitor and past president of U.S. Synchronized Swimming. The RLS also published a book which described how to do the stunts and how to scull, the fundamental method of propulsion in synchronized swimming. In 1898 the Canadian Royal Life Saving Society, also all-male, had a similar exhibition of stunt swimming.

In the early 1900s, Annette Kellerman, the legendary Australian swimmer, demonstrated water ballet moves in glass tanks of water on stages all over the United States and Europe. During these exhibitions Kellerman took the bold move of wearing a form-fitting silk swimsuit instead of the voluminous dress-with-pantaloons "bathing costume" that proper ladies were expected to wear. Crowds gathered as much to see her daring swimsuit as to admire her extraordinary prowess in the water, but nevertheless, Kellerman helped make women's swimming acceptable.

From Ballet to Synchro by Way of Vaudeville

Katherine Curtis, a student and diver at the University of Wisconsin, began to combine some of the RLS's stunts with water ballet and diving moves in the water. "She actually had a vaudeville coach work with her," says Dawn Pawson Bean. "Curtis started a women's swim club at the university in 1917, the year she graduated, but she stayed at Wisconsin for a while, and in 1920, they held a water pageant at the university." Bean goes on to say that by 1923 Curtis was developing "rhythmic swimming" at the University of Chicago, putting together routines of strokes, stunts, and floats (in which the swimmers float on the surface and make a pattern), and setting those routines to music. "Before that, the coach stood on the deck and blew a whistle to let the swimmers know it was time to do a new position. Adding music is Curtis's—and America's—great contribution to synchro." [16]

Another great American contribution was in naming the sport. In 1934 thirty of Curtis's students put on three shows a day at the Chicago World's Fair, performing as the Modern Mermaids. The announcer for the show was former swim champion Norman Ross, and it was he who began to call the routines "synchronized swimming." Curtis moved along to two other Chicago colleges, starting synchronized groups at both schools. In 1937 one team proposed a competition with the other, and the first synchronized swimming meet was held in Chicago on May 29, 1939.

By that time the Midwest states director of the Amateur Athletic Union (AAU), D. Clark Leach, decided that synchronized swimming would be a good addition to swimming and diving meets. He asked

Curtis to draw up rules of competition, and the national AAU accepted synchro as a competitive sport late in 1940. However, the first official national championship, delayed by World War II, was not held until 1946. At first it was a team-only competition, but in 1950, solo events were added.

Meanwhile, the sport was also developing in Canada, though in a different way. "Canadian synchronized swimming in the early years put more emphasis on grace, and less on speed, than the American approach did," says Dawn Pawson Bean.[17] When the first Canadian national competition was held in 1948, it was for solos only; duets and team events were added in the next two years.

International Attention

Canadian and American synchronized swimmers quickly put their sport on the map with exhibition swims at the inaugural Pan American Games in 1951 and the 1952 Helsinki Olympics. This led to the sport starting up in other nations, and synchronized swimming was accepted as a legitimate aquatic sport by the international sanctioning body, FINA. However, says Bean, "Synchro had a long way to go to get recognized as an Olympic sport. Lots of people thought it was more like a water show than a sport."[18]

Technical rules were drawn up for international competition, and the first

THE ARTISTIC SIDE OF SYNCHRO

The International Academy of Aquatic Art (IAAA) owes its existence to a disagreement the synchronized swimming community had back in the 1950s. Synchro was beginning to be contested in international competitions such as the Pan American Games, but the leaders of the sport knew that real respectability would not come until it was an Olympic event. They looked at the rules and every aspect of synchronized swimming competition and decided that the best way to demonstrate the seriousness and athleticism of the sport was to be very precise about the rules and the way it was swum.

However, a large group of people in the sport believed that the real heart of synchronized swimming was its artistry rather than its athleticism. They were so opposed to the direction that the sport was taking that they withdrew and formed the International Academy of Aquatic Art. Today, nine clubs—mostly concentrated in the Chicago area—send teams to annual competitions. There also are a few foreign groups which participate. Presentations at IAAA meetings are based on standard synchro movements, but from there they branch into productions with themes and costumes that are much more theatrical than those done at international and Olympic competitions. U.S. Synchro competitors occasionally take part in IAAA meets; most notably in recent years, male star Bill May presented and performed his original solo, "Mortal Body." However, far fewer people participate in this artistic side of the sport, and it is likely to remain a tiny, niche sport for the foreseeable future.

multination competition for solos, duets, and teams was held at the 1955 Pan American Games in Mexico City. Unfortunately, the new rules led to a split in the synchronized swimming community in the United States. Bean explains, "So the rules that were revised in 1956 were very rigid about what you could and could not do. It didn't leave much room for creativity, which led to a group which felt that synchro was meant to be artistic and creative, [who] split off and formed the International Academy of Aquatic Art. Synchro was a really small sport then, and when you lose literally half your people, it's hard to keep on."[19]

But a small group, mostly women fully dedicated to the sport, kept on. When the first world swimming championships were held in 1973 in Belgrade, synchronized swimming was included. Then in 1977 the U.S. Congress disbanded the AAU, and the sport got its own national sanctioning body, U.S. Synchronized Swimming, also known as Synchro Swimming USA. Bean was elected its first president, a post which is still held by volunteers. Synchronized swimming made its Olympic debut at the 1984 Los Angeles Games, with solo and duet events only.

At the time, America's best synchronized swimmers were Tracy Ruiz and Candie Costie, who had been competing both against each other and as a duet team since 1975. At first the Olympic competition was scheduled to be only a duet event, but just a few months before the Games a solo event was added. Each swimmer quickly developed a solo to present along with their routine together. Ruiz took the gold and Costie the silver in the solos, and together they won the duet.

Solo and duet medals were awarded at the 1988 and 1992 Games, but these events were dropped in favor of eight-member team competition at the 1996 Atlanta Olympics. The duet was restored for the 2000 Sydney Games, however.

Canadian and American teams dominated the sport in the 1980s and 1990s. After Ruiz, the top swimmer in the late 1980s was Canada's Carolyn Waldo. However, at the 1996 Olympics and in the qualifying meets leading up to it, the United States was the runaway champion. At the 1995 Olympic qualifying meet, the U.S. team made history by scoring the first perfect tens in the history of international synchronized swimming competition. They went on to win gold at the Atlanta Games. Russian Anna Koslova was the best individual swimmer of the early 1990s but felt held back by her home team and the lack of top-level coaching in the former Soviet Union. She immigrated to the United States in the mid-1990s and became a citizen just in time to swim for the United States in Sydney.

The Olympics provided a highly visible platform for the sport, which boosted interest and participation all over the world.

Candie Costie and Tracy Ruiz break into tears during the Star Spangled Banner after they receive gold medals at the 1984 Olympics.

The Olympics are limited to eight competing countries, and have included only teams from the United States, Canada, Mexico, France, Japan, Russia, China, and Italy; however, teams from many more countries compete in other international meets. The added TV exposure from the Olympics earned synchronized swimmers a lot of respect for the high level of fitness and athleticism necessary to meet the extraordinary demands of the sport.

Synchro Basics

The fundamentals of synchronized swimming have not changed much since the 1950s. Competitions must be held in deep pools—nine feet of water is the minimum depth allowed. The water has to be deep to allow for the various stunts and to ensure that the swimmers feet or hands do not touch the bottom. Touching the bottom or walls of the pool is against the rules in competition and will cost a team or swimmer points.

At a competition, swimmers may have to perform a technical program, a free routine, and a figure competition or some combination of two out of the three. Technical routines require that a set of basic, standard actions are performed simultaneously by a duet or team. A figure competition requires each swimmer to show her individual mastery of several figures, which are a series of standard movements woven together. A free routine, which can be performed by a solo, duet, or team, allows the swimmers to put together moves, strokes, and stunts to interpret a theme and to show off their strengths.

The nineteen basic positions that synchronized swimmers can choose from have been set since the 1940s. Some positions are done on the surface, either prone or on the back, some are done with much—and in some cases, all—of the body submerged, with only part of one or

The debut of synchronized swimming at the 1984 Olympics boosted the prestige and popularity of a sport long denigrated by many competitive swimmers.

The artistry of synchronized swimming lies in the highly technical and simultaneous movement of the swimmers.

both legs above the surface. Many positions are done upside down, with the swimmers' heads underwater for up to a minute.

In all the basic positions the toes must be pointed, the legs, trunk, and neck fully extended unless the rules specify another way, and the body must meet the water surface at prescribed places. These are among the technical points on which the swimmers are judged. Technical judges also look for all the moves to be done simultaneously by every swimmer; the duet or team must move as one with the music. The artistry in a performance comes from the way the swimmers move from one position to another and present the moves as a coherent performance.

Not as Easy as It Looks

Synchronized swimming moves must look effortless, fluid, and graceful, but achieving that illusion demands mastery of several underwater skills that require concentration and stamina. Swimmers achieve this only through long hours of practice. Probably the most fundamental skill is controlled breathing. In a five-minute routine, an elite synchro swimmer may be underwater for a full minute. This means she has to learn to inhale forcefully and exhale properly. Synchro swimmers do not really "hold" their breath; they learn to exhale slowly through their mouths while they are underwater, timing it to the split second so they finish breathing out just as they break the surface.

The most necessary piece of equipment for a synchronized swimmer is not her vivid lipstick, her hair gel, or her sequins. It is her nose clip. The clip is vital for keeping water out of the swimmer's nose while she is upside down underwater; it also helps control her breathing. The nose clip is so important that many swimmers keep a spare somewhere in their swimsuit in case the first one is knocked off during a routine.

Since synchronized swimmers cannot touch the bottom or walls, they have to create the illusion that they are standing on their feet or hands. And in fact, the techniques for this—eggbeatering with the legs and sculling with the hands and arms—allow swimmers to use the force of the water to move or keep still. In eggbeatering, the swimmer moves her legs in a series of small, intersecting circles; in sculling, she uses her flat palms and forearms in a figure eight pattern. Each technique requires a good "feel" for the water and a well-developed sense of how to hold a position while floating.

The third fundamental skill is balance. Many athletic people seem to have an inborn sense of "proprioception" or the ability to know where each part of their body is. Others have to learn it. This can be done by drills which focus on balance in

DAVE BARRY SWALLOWS HIS SCORN AND A LOT OF POOL WATER

"There's an old saying in journalism: 'Be careful of what you make fun of, because you could find yourself upside down attempting a Vertical Split while your lungs rapidly fill with water,'" Dave Barry wrote in *Dave Barry Is From Venus and Mars*. The nationally syndicated humor columnist had leveled several of his not-so-gentle gibes at synchro over the years, so in retaliation (says Barry) he was invited to work out with the U.S. Synchronized Swimming National Team One shortly before the 1996 Olympics.

Barry and his *Miami Herald* colleague Dan Le Batard found that those fixed smiles on synchro swimmers are, in fact, genuine—at least when they are pointed at two sputtering middle-aged male media types. Barry also found that his body "hurtles directly for the pool bottom" despite all his attempts to learn sculling or eggbeating. He further found out that getting any part of his leg higher than his toes out of the water was next to impossible.

"Anyway, after about 45 straight minutes of alternately eggbeatering and sinking, I came to the surface, and, using what little air I had left in my lungs, shouted: 'THIS IS THE HARDEST SPORT IN THE WORLD!' Then, and only then," he wrote contritely, "did they let us out of the pool."

the water, using the buoyancy of the lungs to "lean" on in the water. Balance drills also serve to make sure that the swimmer can stroke and turn as strongly on her non-dominant side as on her favored one. Much of the dryland training that synchro swimmers do—weight training and calisthenics, for example—is geared at strengthening their "core" muscles in their torsos, since this is where balance and power in the water begin.

Core strength is not needed just for balance, however. In lift movements, where one swimmer is held above the surface by one or more of the others, the supporting swimmers can use only their own muscle power.

It takes many hours of intense practice to hone all of these skills as well as the perfect coordination of each move. Elite teams practice six or eight hours a day, six days a week. Even recreational and age-group teams put in between six and twelve hours of practice a week.

Once a top-caliber synchronized swimmer's competitive career is over, there are not many professional opportunities. Coaching and teaching are the most common options. There are occasional "aquacades" mounted for special events like World's Fairs and occasional touring shows similar to ice skating shows. Water shows have become increasingly popular in the large hotels in Las Vegas. Throughout the 1990s the Riviera Hotel featured a show called *Splash*, which starred former U.S. and world champion Linda Shelley. And the biggest water show in history, the Cirque du Soleil's *O* at the Renaissance Hotel in Las Vegas, is both directed by, and stars, the Canadian champion Sylvie Frechette. Breaking all records for both extravagance and attendance in Las Vegas, *O* shows that there is an enormous attraction to the artistic side of swimming.

CHAPTER 6

Stars of Swimming

Every decade of the twentieth century saw swimming records broken and new stars of the sport emerge. Radio, newsreels, movies, and finally, television, made champion swimmers into celebrities. Many used their fame to achieve success and prominence in other fields, not all of which related to swimming or even sports. Others simply enjoyed their time at the top, then retired to take up "normal" life.

Each of the following swimmers were arguably the dominant figures of the sport at their times. Their lives after swimming differ greatly from each other, but as a group, swimmers tend to do well in later life. This may be due to the discipline and self-esteem that long years of intense swim training can foster; it may also be

because most swimmers have also had the benefits of comfortable, middle-class up-bringings and good educations. Most likely, it is because the best swimmers must learn to call on all their determination and mental toughness to succeed—thus they become people who are not easily daunted by life's often harsh realities.

Johnny Weissmuller

For the first half of the twentieth century, Johnny Weissmuller epitomized swimming. In a ten-year career as an amateur, Weissmuller broke sixty-seven world records, won five gold medals in two Olympics (1924, 1928), won fifty-two national championships, and never lost a race. He was simply unbeatable.

SWIMMERS WHO BECAME STARS

Some swimming champions stroked their way to Hollywood stardom. The three most famous were Johnny Weismuller, Buster Crabbe, and Esther Williams.

Weissmuller *was* Tarzan for moviegoers. His long straight hair, high cheekbones, and wide mouth, paired with a broad chest and long, muscular legs, made him the ape-man personified. Weissmuller had at least one swimming scene in every movie, and Tarzan often saved the day by swimming to the rescue. Weissmuller played a few other roles in his Hollywood years, but was always careful to present a public image of the heroic jungle man.

Clarence "Buster" Crabbe burst onto the American swimming scene at the 1932 Los Angeles Olympics. A week after winning a dramatic 400-meter race (the only medal not won by the Japanese men's team), Paramount Pictures signed the handsome blond to a hundred-dollar-a-week contract. Renamed Buster, Crabbe went on to make nearly two hundred movies and eight famous film serials, including *Flash Gordon* and *Buck Rogers*. At the height of his career, Crabbe was one of the biggest stars in the movies.

The swimming star who epitomized the sport for Americans is Esther Williams. A champion swimmer by the age of fifteen, and at sixteen the first female American

American actor and Olympic swimmer Johnny Weissmuller treks through the jungle in his role as Tarzan.

butterfly champion, Williams lost her chance for Olympic glory when war canceled the 1940 Olympics. A stint in the Billy Rose Aquacade brought her the attention of MGM Studios, where she soon became a star. Every one of her twenty-four movies centered on her swimming—and so did her carefully planned retirement. Williams started a swimming pool company in the late 1950s which made backyard pools accessible for millions of Americans. Widowed in the early 1980s, she took up swimsuit design and is still involved in that business. And, she still swims.

Weissmuller was six feet, three inches tall, weighed 190 pounds, and had the classic swimmer physique—broad shoulders and chest, long limbs, and large feet. He was blessed with an abundance of natural talent, the drive and determination to practice for endless hours, and one of the best of the early coaches, "Big Bill" Bachrach. Weissmuller's hydroplaning style was unconventional—head and shoulders held high, back arched, and feet low in the water are the opposite of any ideas of hydrodynamics. Yet he was blindingly fast—his

record in the 100-yard freestyle, 51 seconds, stood for seventeen years. In 1937, at the age of thirty-six, he swam the 100-meter in an unofficial 48.5, which stood for thirty-nine years.

By that time, Weissmuller was comfortable with the Hollywood set as well as the racing pool. He had parlayed his swimming fame into the perfect role for him—Tarzan. In the multitude of movies about the heroic ape-man, Weissmuller did not do much other than look good, swim strongly, act manly, and speak broken English. But

CLASH OF THE TITANS

The 1924 Paris Olympics witnessed one of the great torch-passing events in swimming history. Lined up on the starting blocks for the 100-meter freestyle were the legendary Duke Kahanamoku, a record holder and Olympic champion for twelve years, and Johnny Weissmuller, his challenger and the current record holder.

Kahanamoku was thirty. He, almost more than any other person, was responsible for the alternating overarm technique of freestyle, or crawl. For him it was natural—the way generations of his ancestors had stroked through the waves of his native Hawaii. His runaway success with the stroke, beginning at the 1912 Olympics, destroyed all rationale for any other crawl technique.

Weissmuller was twenty. He had already beaten the old master twice—once in a 100-yard straightaway grudge match in Hawaii and again in a preliminary meet in Indianapolis, where Weissmuller set a new record (59.25 seconds) that was

a full second faster than the Duke's 1920 Olympic mark.

Weissmuller was confident, but nervous. Kahanamoku could not only call on his experience, but his brother Sam was in the next lane. But while they walked to the pool deck, Kahanamoku smiled at the younger man. "Good luck, Johnny," he said. "The most important thing is to get the American flag up there three times. Let's do it!"

At the gun, Weissmuller took off like a shot and won easily, setting a new Olympic record (59.0) in the process. The real race was between the Kahanamokus, with Duke edging his brother for second place with a time of 1:00.25; Sam came in at 1:01.45.

It was a stirring race, though it effectively ended Duke's career as a sprinter. He went back to surfing in Hawaii and gained some fame as a movie actor. Weissmuller went on to be the best swimmer of the first half of the twentieth century.

it was enough for movie audiences around the world, and he set the standard for subsequent movie Tarzans.

Adolph Keifer

At seventeen, Adolph Keifer was the youngest member of the U.S. Olympic team at the 1936 Berlin Games, but he already had several international races under his belt and held the record for the 100-yard backstroke, 57.6 seconds. One year earlier, he had become the first person to break the one-minute mark in that event. Nevertheless, Keifer and his teammates were considered underdogs to the Japanese team which had won virtually every medal at the previous Olympics.

Keifer's backstroke technique, which was adopted around the world as the most efficient backstroke method for more than twenty years, had three unique features. He used a straight-arm recovery swung low over the water (instead of the windmill action that had been common), a catch (entry) wide of the shoulder instead of in line with it, and a straight-arm pull, just beneath the surface instead of deep in the water.

During the backstroke events of the 1936 Olympics, Keifer broke his world record in the 100-meter preliminaries, then repeated the feat in the semifinals, and destroyed it again in the final with a time of 1:05.90. It was one of only two gold medals the United States took in swimming that year, but it signaled the complete eclipse of the Japanese swimmers.

Even after the end of Keifer's competitive career, he remained an influential figure in swimming and water sports. His company, Adolph Keifer and Associates, has pioneered many innovations in swim and pool gear, such as wave-dampening lane lines. Keifer's business, which he still actively supervises, is one of the largest pool, water therapy, and aquatic equipment concerns in the world.

Murray Rose

Australian Murray Rose grew up swimming in the ocean and tidal pools of Sydney. He shot to fame at age sixteen as the youngest man to win Olympic gold, winning three medals at the 1956 Games in Melbourne. Four years later at the Rome Olympics, he became the first man to win distance events in two successive Games.

Rose is considered by many swimming experts to be the best swimmer of all times. He competed at the top levels of the sport and held records for nine years, from 1955 to 1964, one of the longest careers at the top of competitive swimming. Most of Rose's records were set at the long end of the swimming spectrum, the 400-meter, the 800, and the 1,500 (known as the metric mile) as well as the 440-yard, the 880, and the 1,600. But unlike many distance specialists,

Rose could also sprint the short races and held the 200-meter freestyle record as well.

Rose immigrated to the United States in the early 1960s and graduated from the University of Southern California. He took up acting and television sports commentary and was affiliated for many years with the Los Angeles Forum, the arena which used to be home to the Lakers. He still races occasionally in Masters Swimming competition and holds several world Masters records.

In the early 1990s, the Irish scholar Charles Sprawson swam with Rose, who was his childhood idol. Sprawson writes in his academic treatise on swimming, *Haunts of the Black Masseur: The Swimmer as Hero*, that Rose "still looked much as he did in his prime, and . . . had the long hands and feet that all the best swimmers seem to possess."[20] Rose easily beat Sprawson, who is more than ten years younger, in an informal race; in fact, at that time Rose was swimming some events faster than he had done in his Olympic years.

For Rose, swimming is an intensely sensuous experience, writes Sprawson, and he believes that a "feel" for the water is the prime ingredient for swimming success. It was Rose who brought the Australian swimmers' custom of shaving their legs to the United States, where it quickly evolved into a whole-body pre-race ritual. This may be Murray Rose's most lasting legacy to his sport.

Donna De Varona

One of the crop of very young champions, Donna De Varona made the 1960 U.S. Olympic team at the age of thirteen. That was a big year for her—she set the world record (5:36.5) in the individual medley and reset the record the following year. She also set records in backstroke; her time in the 100-meter backstroke was 1:08.9. At the 1964 Olympics in Tokyo, De Varona, a veteran at seventeen, won the first gold medal in women's individual medley with a time of 5:18.7. She also won a gold as part of the women's freestyle relay.

In addition to Olympic medals, De Varona won numerous sports awards. By the time she was eighteen, she had been named America's Outstanding Athlete by the Associated Press and the Greatest Woman Athlete by the National Association of Swimmers. But her swimming career was over when De Varona retired from racing to attend college.

Following graduation, she became television's first woman sportscaster, taking a job with ABC's *Wide World of Sports*. "Little did I know as I stood on the [medal] platform at the Tokyo Olympics, that only my Olympic experience could have prepared me for what was to come," remembers De Varona.[21] Later, De Varona

Donna De Varona swims the butterfly in the 200-yard individual medley at the National AAU championships in 1964.

was one of the most influential voices pushing for the passage of Title IX, the federal funding statute which sought to equalize athletic opportunities for women in colleges. De Varona continues to work for ABC and has been a leader in many women's sports organizations.

Mark Spitz

Clearly the best male swimmer of the second half of the twentieth century, Mark Spitz made swimming the glamour sport of the 1970s. Millions of people who could not name another swimmer hung his famous poster on their walls (the second best-selling poster in history, after Betty Grable's), and for several years, Spitz's gleaming smile promoted dozens of products. He made it look easy, but Mark Spitz worked very hard for his fame.

Spitz's ability was apparent very early, especially to his father, who organized his family's life around Mark's swimming career. Spitz had the advantage of excellent coaching from his early years and was setting records by the time he was ten. He won his first national championship at age seventeen. The following year, he set six world records in the lead-up to the Mexico City Olympics, but was disappointed to win "only" two gold medals, both in relay events.

Following the Olympics he entered Indiana University, where he joined the swimming team coached by the legendary James "Doc" Counsilman. In college Spitz became one of the NCAA's most dominant swimmers, known almost as much for his single-minded determination and drive as for his monumental talent.

Spitz himself became a legend at the 1972 Munich Olympic Games. After announcing that he would win a gold medal in each of the seven events he was entered in, Spitz did it. Setting world records in each event, Spitz won more gold medals than any Olympian in history, in any sport.

The night after his final event, Palestinian terrorists infiltrated the Olympic Village, killing two Israeli athletes and taking nine more hostage. As the crisis spun out over several days, U.S. Olympics officials feared that Spitz, who is Jewish, was also a potential target. So he was spirited out of Germany and back home to both adulation and inquiries he was unprepared to answer.

"All of a sudden I'm being asked about terrorists," says Spitz. "I had Jewish people approach me about my posturing, and my lack of posturing. I was 22 years old. What was I gonna say? I thought it was the most terrible thing that ever happened at the Olympics."[22]

DOC COUNSILMAN: SCIENTIST, COACH, CHANNEL SWIMMER

James "Doc" Counsilman was the preeminent coach of the twentieth century. His statistics are awe inspiring: His Indiana University team was unbeaten for twelve seasons, winning twenty straight Big Ten conference titles. His team produced forty-eight Olympians who won forty-six medals, among them Mark Spitz, Don Schollander, Chet Jastremski, and Gary Hall Sr. He was coach of the U.S. men's Olympic teams twice, in 1964 and 1976, when his teams crushed the rest of the world's best swimmers.

Counsilman combined brilliant stroke analysis with iron discipline, inspiration, and strong paternalism. He was the first coach to use underwater still photography and to apply the principles of fluid mechanics to swimming. His swimmers were the first to take up weight lifting and have classroom instruction. His innovations in stroke technique revolutionized swimming, and his book, *The Science of Swimming*, was translated into twenty languages. "The whole growth of swimming internationally was because of Doc's unselfishness," Chet Jastremski said in the April/May 1997 issue of *Rodale's Fitness Swimmer*. "He wasn't one of those guys who tried to keep his training techniques and stroke theories secret from the rest of the world."

Not content with coaching and inspiring young swimmers, Counsilman trained hard, and at the age of fifty-eight in 1979 became the oldest person to swim the English Channel. "I want to lead a gray revolution to fitness for older people," he said at the time. Unfortunately, his own fitness could not stave off the effects of Parkinson's disease. Now in his eighties, Counsilman lives in retired seclusion in Indiana.

Mary T. Meagher jets through the water at a 1979 butterfly event.

After the 1972 Olympics, Spitz abandoned his swimming career. With his life and ego entirely identified with swimming, Spitz was ill-prepared for life out of the swimming limelight. "I don't have a made-for-TV, up-close-and-personal personality,"[23] he says. Used to the steady stroking and support of his family and coaches, Spitz reacted to negative comments in the press by becoming withdrawn and uncooperative. Nevertheless, his fame and good looks paved the way for lucrative years making TV commercials and doing product endorsements.

At the age of forty-one, married and the father of two sons, Spitz attempted an unsuccessful comeback to Olympic swimming. He missed the cutoff time to qualify for the 100-meter butterfly (55.59) at the 1992 U.S. Olympic Trials by nearly three seconds. Spitz still trains with the UCLA Masters team, but that is now his only connection with swimming.

Mary T. Meagher

Mary T. Meagher was the tenth of eleven children, and the second named Mary. To distinguish herself from her older sister, Mary Glen, she was called Mary T.

Mary T. came at the end of the run of very young champions—she was only fifteen when, in August 1981, she set an astonishing set of butterfly records which stood for twenty years. On August 13 she set her fifth world record with a time of 2:05.96 in the 200-meter butterfly. On August 16 she shattered her own 100 butterfly record to 57.93. No other woman broke 59 seconds in that event until 1990. *Sports Illustrated* rates her feat as the fifth-greatest single-event record of all time in any sport—only records set by Wilt Chamberlain, Secretariat, Bob Beamon, and Norm Van Brocklin were ahead of this self-described "naive" teenager.

Yet despite her consistent record-breaking performances, "Madame Butterfly" remains less known than many less accomplished swimmers. Part of this is because the height of her career came during the years when first the United States, then the Soviet Union and the Eastern bloc boycotted the Olympic Games. It was not until Seoul in 1988 that Meagher swam against the world's other top swimmers. But by then she was twenty-three, struggling to overcome an eating disorder, and operating under the mind-set that she was "too old." She retired after the Olympics and says she has no regrets. Still, she says, "I think if I had made some different decisions when I got older, I could have reset my world records." [24]

As it was, the last one did not fall until 1999, when twenty-six-year-old American Jenny Thompson reset it at 57.88 seconds at the Pan Pacific Championships. By then Madame Butterfly was Mrs. Plant, a suburban wife and mother whose last brush with Olympic fame was to carry the Olympic flag into the stadium at the 1996 Atlanta Games. "Swimming isn't nearly as much my identity anymore," she admits. "It used to be an ace in my pocket when I wanted it, like for a job or an ego boost. It's not anymore. My ace in my pocket now is my daughter and my husband." [25]

Amy Van Dyken

Amy Van Dyken is swimming's Cinderella. Struck by life-threatening asthma when she was a baby, Van Dyken was denied a normal childhood. Her asthma, which could be triggered by exercise, by a host of allergens, or by an illness, kept her from doing anything but the most passive playing. Her illness interrupted school frequently, not that she really minded. At school, Van Dyken was teased and picked on because of her frailty, and later because of her height (she reached her full six feet before the age of fourteen).

Unlike many top swimmers, Van Dyken did not show any promise in the pool as a child. When she was six, a doctor suggested swimming as a way to exercise in conditions that were less likely to cause an asthma attack. But until she was a

Amy Van Dyken competes at the 1996 Atlanta Olympics where she received four gold medals.

junior in high school, Van Dyken was such a slow swimmer she was nearly dropped from her high school team. Then, at seventeen, her years of practice and determination began to pay off. She set several school swim records and won a scholarship to Arizona State University.

At Arizona State, she took second place in the 50-yard freestyle race at the NCAA national championships. Transferring to Colorado State, she was named NCAA Female Swimmer of the Year in 1994. In 1995 she dropped out to join the U.S. resident swim team, where coach Jonty Skinner taught her how to harness her mental toughness and maintain speed to the end of a race. The breakthrough was dramatic.

After winning gold medals and setting records in both freestyle and butterfly at the Pan American Games, Van Dyken became one of the brightest stars of the 1996 Olympics. In Atlanta she became the first American woman to win four gold medals in a single Games; she also set two new records. Within days, Van Dyken was the center of massive media attention. Apart from appearances on virtually every major talk show, she posed for a number of advertisement campaigns, most memorably,

"Got Milk?" Van Dyken went on to win three gold medals at the 1998 World Championship, despite a severely injured shoulder. Several rounds of surgery failed to get her back into competitive shape, so Van Dyken retired after the 2000 Games in Sydney. Now married to Tom Rouen, the punter for the Denver Broncos, Van Dyken is the spokesperson for Athletes with Asthma and Paws with a Cause, a group which trains dogs to assist deaf people.

The Rewards of Swimming

Swimmers, coaches, and swimming science researchers have improvised, devised, and tested hundreds of subtle changes to increase speed and efficiency—the angle of a hand, the flex of a foot, the cut of a swimsuit. The swimmers and coaches profiled here are just a small fraction of the people who have made significant contributions to the sport in the past century. Not all of the innovators became famous, even inside the sport, but they have all shared the satisfaction of making a difference for swimming and other swimmers.

Satisfaction is a constant theme when people involved in swimming talk about their sport. Swimming is personally rewarding for nearly everyone who participates, from Olympic stars to fitness swimmers. Swimmers say it gives them a host of physical, mental, psychological, and even spiritual benefits. "My wife (Sandy Neilsen) won three Olympic golds," says Masters competitor and sports psychologist Keith Bell. "I've never won a race anywhere near that level. But Sandy never got any more out of swimming than I do. Swimming is a richly rewarding experience that you can have every day of your life." [26]

Awards and Statistics

Federation Internationale
de Natation Amateur (FINA)
World Records

Men

Style	Swimmer	Nation	Time	Date	Place
50 FREE	Alexander Popov	Russia	0:21.64	June 16, 2000	Moscow, Russia
100 FREE	Pieter van den Hoogenband	Netherlands	0:47.84	September 19, 2000	Sydney, Australia
50 BACK	Lenny Krayzelburg	United States	0:24.99	August 28, 1999	Sydney, Australia
100 BACK	Lenny Krayzelburg	United States	0:53.60	August 24, 1999	Sydney, Australia
50 BREAST	Oleg Lisogor	Ukraine	0:27.18	August 2, 2002	Berlin, Germany
100 BREAST	Roman Sloudnov	Russia	0:59.94	July 23, 2001	Fukuoka, Japan
50 FLY	Geoffrey Huegill	Australia	0:23.44	July 27, 2001	Fukuoka, Japan
100 FLY	Michael Klim	Australia	0:51.81	December 12, 1999	Canberra, Australia

Relays

Style	Team	Time	Date	Place
4 x 100 MED	United States	03:33.48	August 29, 2002	Yokohama, Japan
Aaron Peirsol		0:54.17		
Brendon Hansen		1:54.31		
Michael Phelps		2:45.44		
Jason Lezak		3:33.48		

.

Women

Style	Swimmer	Nation	Time	Date	Place
50 FREE	Inge de Bruijn	Netherlands	0:24.13	September 22, 2000	Sydney, Australia
100 FREE	Inge de Bruijn	Netherlands	0:53.77	September 20, 2000	Sydney, Australia
50 BACK	Sandra Voelker	Germany	0:28.25	June 17, 2000	Berlin, Germany
100 BACK	Cihong He	China	1:00.16	September 10, 1994	Rome, Italy
50 BREAST	Zoe Baker	Great Britain	0:30.57*	July 30, 2002	Manchester, Great Britain
100 BREAST	Penelope Heyns	Republic of South Africa	1:06.52	August 23, 1999	Canberra, Australia
50 FLY	Ana-Karin Kammerling	Sweden	0:25.57	July 30, 2000	Berlin, Germany
100 FLY	Inge de Bruijn	Netherlands	0:56.61	September 17, 2000	Sydney, Australia

* to be ratified by FINA Honorary Secretary

Relays

Style	Team	Time	Date	Place
4x100 MEDLEY	United States	3:58.30	September 23, 2000	Sydney, Australia
B. J. Bedford		1:01.39		
Megan Quann		1:06.29		
Jenny Thompson		0:57.25		
Dara Torres		0:53.37		

Source: FINA website, September 13, 2002. www.fina.org.

Notes

Chapter 1: The Evolution of Competitive Swimming

1. Cecil Colwin, *Breakthrough Swimming*. Champaign, IL: Human Kinetics, 2002, pp. 17–18.
2. Colwin, *Breakthrough Swimming*, p. 42.
3. Quoted in Dick Hannula and Nat Thornton, eds., *The Swim Coaching Bible*. Champaign, IL: Human Kinetics, 2001, p. 298.
4. Terry Laughlin, "Short Story," *Rodale's Swimmer*, May/June 2001, pp. 40–41.
5. Hannula and Thornton, *The Swim Coaching Bible*, p. 152.

Chapter 2: Extreme Swimming: Open Water Races and Solo Swims

6. Marcia Cleveland, *Dover Solo*. New York: MMJ Press, 1997, p. 124.

Chapter 3: Women Jump into Swimming

7. Quoted in Karen Christensen et al., eds., *International Encyclopedia of Women and Sports, vol.3*. New York: Macmillan Reference USA, 2000, p. 1134.
8. Quoted in Pat Bigold, "Hall of Fame to Honor Spring-board Legend," *Honolulu Star-Bulletin*, June 6, 2000.
9. Quoted in Bernadette Sukley, "Caught You Peaking," *Rodale's Swimmer*, May/June 2001, p. 60.
10. Quoted in Mel Goldstein and Dave Tanner, *Swimming Past 50*. Champaign, IL: Human Kinetics, 1999, p. 80.

Chapter 4: Doping: Swimming's Biggest Scandal

11. Ray Essick, telephone interview with author, October 2002.
12. Quoted on *20-20*, ABC television, July 18, 2000.
13. Megan Quann, telephone interview with author, October 2002.
14. Quoted in Stephen Harris, "Steroids: A Growing Global Problem," *Rodale's Fitness Swimmer*, Summer 1996, pp. 72–73.
15. Quann, telephone interview.

Chapter 5: Synchronized Swimming

16. Dawn Pawson Bean, telephone interview with author, July 2002.
17. Bean, telephone interview.
18. Bean, telephone interview.
19. Bean, telephone interview.

Chapter 6: Stars of Swimming

20. Charles Sprawson, *Haunts of the Black Masseur: The Swimmer as Hero.* New York: Pantheon, 1992, p. 12.
21. Donna De Varona, "Golden Moments," *Rodale's Fitness Swimmer*, Summer 1996, p. 104.
22. Quoted in Joel Silverman, "The Man Behind the Medals," *Rodale's Fitness Swimmer*, Summer 1996, p. 61.
23. Quoted in Silverman, "The Man Behind the Medals," p. 61.
24. Quoted in Karen Rosen, "Madame Butterfly," *Rodale's Fitness Swimmer*, August/September 1997, p. 62.
25. Quoted in Rosen, "Madame Butterfly," p. 63.
26. Quoted in Martha Capwell Fox, "Extinguishing Burnout," *Splash*, May/June 2002, p. 27.

For Further Reading

Charles Carson Jr., *Make the Team: Swimming and Diving.* New York: Time, 1991. Describes the basic skills, common strokes, dives, and training exercises in competitive swimming and diving.

Rick Cross, *Swimming.* New York: DK Publishing, 2000. Well-illustrated introduction to swimming, showing stroke techniques and basic equipment.

Paula Edelson, *Superstars of Men's Swimming and Diving.* Philadelphia: Chelsea House, 1999. Brief biographies of the top male swimmers and divers of the late 1990s.

Diana Gleasner, *Women in Sports: Swimming.* New York: Harvey House, 1975. Dated but inspiring book directed at girls who swim.

Emmet Hines, *Fitness Swimming.* Champaign, IL: Human Kinetics, 1999. Drills and training programs for fitness swimmers by one of the top-rated coaches in the United States.

Terry Laughlin, *Swimming Made Easy.* New Paltz, NY: Swimware, 2001. Laughlin's somewhat controversial swimming techniques focus on balance and whole-body propulsion in the water; once mastered, however, this is an efficient, comfortable way to swim.

Summer Sanders, *Champions Are Raised, Not Born: How My Parents Made Me a Success.* New York: Delacorte, 1999. Autobiography of a "problem child" who became a champion because of her parents' wisdom.

Barry Wilner, *Swimming.* Austin, TX: Raintree Streck-Vaughn, 1996. Good basic how-to introduction to competitive swimming.

Works Consulted

Books

Dave Barry, *Dave Barry Is From Venus and Mars* New York: Crown Publishing, 1997. A collection of the humorist's favorite newspaper columns from the mid-1990s.

Karen Christensen et al., eds., *International Encyclopedia of Women and Sports.* Vol. 3. New York: Macmillan Reference USA, 2000. Brief but detailed histories of women in distance, marathon, speed, and synchronized swimming, with discussions of techniques, rules, and competition in each aspect of swimming.

Marcia Cleveland, *Dover Solo.* New York: MMJ Press, 1997. Account of Cleveland's preparation for swimming the English Channel and how she reached her goal. One of the best practical how-to books on open water endurance swimming.

Cecil Colwin, *Breakthrough Swimming.* Champaign, IL: Human Kinetics, 2002. A comprehensive and meticulous book on the history of swimming and the evolution of swim technique, by one of the best stroke coaches in the sport.

Penny Lee Dean, *Open Water Swimming.* Champaign, IL: Human Kinetics, 1998. Techniques and training tips interspersed with interesting personal anecdotes, by the women's record holder for the English Channel swim.

Mel Goldstein and Dave Tanner, *Swimming Past 50*, Champaign, IL: Human Kinetics, 1999. Workouts and training programs by two Masters coaches for middle-aged and older swimmers. Primarily aimed at competitors and spiced with inspiring stories of older racers.

Dick Hannula and Nat Thornton, eds., *The Swim Coaching Bible.* Chamapaign, IL: Human Kinetics, 2001. Comprehensive technique and training handbook, written by over two dozen top-level coaches.

Thomas A.P. van Leeuwen, *The Springboard in the Pond.* Cambridge: Massachusetts Institute of Technology Press, 1998. A scholarly but lively and unorthodox history of the swimming pool and its place in human history.

P.J. Muller Jr., *Gold In the Water: The True Story of Ordinary Men and Their Extraordinary Dream of Olympic Glory.* New York: Thomas Dunne, 2001. How two top swimmers trained for the two years leading up to the Sydney Games.

Diana Nyad, *Other Shores.* New York: Random House, 1978. Autobiography of one of America's best open water swimmers.

Charles Sprawson, *Haunts of the Black Masseur: The Swimmer as Hero.* New York: Pantheon, 1992. A scholarly treatise on the history of swimming and its place in human experience.

U.S. Navy Aviation Training Division, *Swimming and Diving.* Annapolis, MD: United States Naval Institute, 1943. World War II–era book of water survival, with details on the military history of swimming and water operations.

Katherine Vaz and Chip Zempel, *Swim, Swim: A Complete Handbook for Fitness Swimmers.* New York: Contemporary Books, 1986. An easy-to-follow how-to book for intermediate swimmers, laced with interesting tips and bits of history and swimming lore.

Conrad Wennerberg, *Wind, Waves, and Sunburn: A Brief History of Marathon Swimming.* New York: Breakaway Books, 1974. Gripping stories of some of the most grueling open water swims in the history of competitive distance swimming; the most comprehensive history of nineteenth- and twentieth-century marathon swimming.

Periodicals

Pat Bigold, "Hall of Fame to Honor Spring-board Legend," *Honolulu Star-Bulletin,* June 6, 2000.

Mary Bolster, "A Swimmer with Heart," *Rodale's Fitness Swimmer,* Fall 1996.

Donna De Varona, "Golden Moments," *Rodale's Fitness Swimmer,* Summer 1996.

Martha Capwell Fox, "Extinguishing Burnout," *Splash,* May/June 2002.

Stephen Harris, "Steroids: A Growing Global Problem," *Rodale's Fitness Swimmer,* Summer 1996.

Jane Katz, "Synch & Swim," *Rodale's Swimmer,* November/December 2000.

Terry Laughlin, "Short Story," *Rodale's Swimmer,* May/June 2001.

Ken McAlpine, "Cold Water, Warm Heart," *Rodale's Fitness Swimmer,* Spring 1996.

Joe Oakes, "Get Off the Rock!" *Rodale's Fitness Swimmer,* July/August 1999.

Karen Rosen, "Madame Butterfly," *Rodale's Fitness Swimmer,* August/September 1997.

Silk, "Review of Silk Knit Goods," March 1915.

Joel Silverman, "From Underdog to Top Dog," *Rodale's Fitness Swimmer,* Winter 1997.

———, "The Luck of the Irish?" *Rodale's Fitness Swimmer,* Winter 1997.

———, "The Man Behind the Medals," *Rodale's Fitness Swimmer,* Summer 1996.

Bernadette Sukley, "Caught You Peaking," *Rodale's Swimmer,* May/June 2001.

Mark Zeigler, "Doc," *Rodale's Fitness Swimmer,* April/May 1997.

Internet Source

Jim Dreyer, Swim For New Horizons. www.swimjimswim.org.

Index

Picture Credits

Cover Photo: © Nick Wilson/Getty Images

© AFP/CORBIS, 53

© Associated Press, AP, 22, 50, 59, 63, 77, 81

© Associated Press, KEYSTONE, 58

© Bettmann/CORBIS, 35, 67

© Corel, 10, 19, 25, 26, 30, 68, 69

© Michael Kevin Daly/CORBIS, 11

© Tony Duffy/Allsport, 79

© Historical Picture Archive/CORBIS, 17

© Hulton/Archive by Getty Images, 33, 37, 41, 43, 45, 73

© Vanni Archive/CORBIS, 14

© Nick Wilson/Getty Images, 47

About the Author

Martha Capwell Fox is a lifelong swimmer and former senior editor of *Rodale's Swimmer* magazine. She has written extensively on swimming, health, and nutrition, as well as on the history of her hometown, Catasauqua, Pennsylvania.